VOICES
OF THE
UNIVERSE

Your voice affects the universe
Let it be with **LOVE**

A Matthew Book with Suzanne Ward

ISBN 9780971787544

Library of Congress 2003112298

Second edition 2011

This book was printed in the United States of America

Cover design by Chooi-Chin Goh, United Kingdom

MATTHEW BOOKS
P. O. Box 1043
Camas, Washington 98607

www.matthewbooks.com
suzy@matthewbooks.com

What is love?

In simplest terms, love is God's sharing of Himself with all of His creations. Love is the healing force of the universe. Love is within the soul and needs only your allowance of those innate sensations of loving others and receiving their love for you. Love has no limitations, no boundaries to its capacity.

In expression, love is treating others with kindness, fairness, honesty, compassion, helpfulness, caring. If love can be said to have "ingredients," then those are some of the ingredients of godly expression in action.

Knowing that you and God and every other of God's creations are inseparable is love. Knowing that Earth is a sentient, conscious life herself and respecting all of her life forms is love. Realizing that no one can know others at soul level and therefore does not judge them but rather does not condone an action seen as injurious, is love.

Listening to one's godself is love. Living the kind of life that engenders loving self is love. Feeling joy yourself when you see it in others is love. Doing something that brings joy to another is love. Forgiveness of self and others is love. Sharing your resources with full heart is love. Doing good deeds without attaching expectations is love.

Feeling peace of heart and mind is love. The quiet thrill of seeing a sunset or hearing a songbird is love, and a smile is one of the simplest and most radiating expressions of love.

In any or all of these instances and many others that you may encounter that instinctively you know are love in action, you are manifesting your love for and of God.

Mother, I don't think I've told you anything at all surprising. But perhaps it is good to have some references as a guiding light in these times when darkness may seem to be overshadowing the magnificent abundance of love that is in your world.

Matthew

VOICES
OF THE
UNIVERSE

CONTENTS

PART IV MORE FROM MATTHEW

PART V OTHER VOICES BEYOND EARTH

PART VI THE POWER OF LOVE

GLOSSARY

OTHER MATTHEW BOOKS

FOREWORD

I was sweeping the deck when I heard "voices of the universe." It was God speaking, and that was to be the title of a new book. *"Your voices as much as any others are 'voices of the universe,' and you need to start thinking of yourselves that way."*

What *I* was thinking was that after a year of turmoil, when only a few hundred copies of the first two books were printed and the press-ready disks were destroyed by the printer, recently I had gotten those books back into production at the same time I was completing the third one. That had been a huge undertaking in time and expense, and my reply to God's new expectation was, "Oh, no!"

"Yes. It has to be out by early next year. Before then would be better."

"Why?"

"My children need to know that this is a critical time, and you are dallying."

"Our garage is filled with cartons of books, and just where will the money come from to print another one?"

"It will be supplied."

I had learned that questioning God is fine—He delights in that and wishes more of us heard His answers—but arguing with Him is futile.

Actually, I had a bit of a head start on the book. Two months before that conversation, Hatonn had given me a message that he said was for "the next book." It was good that his information was timeless, I thought, because I felt sure that a *lot* of time would pass before *anything* would have to be put into a book. But it's as I said, there's no sense arguing with God, and Hatonn's message turned out to be not only timeless, but timely—it got *Voices of the Universe* underway.

Hatonn's voice and those of other high light sources are unquestionably important. *So are ours!* We need to communicate more clearly and sincerely with each other, God said, and because our words, thoughts and deeds affect the entire universe, they need to be based in LOVE so that this most powerful force in the universe flows out from our world to all the rest of His creations.

Since the books and Matthew's messages have become known in more than 40 countries, I have received several thousand e-mails and letters from readers. Some describe their personal losses and the comfort they received from *Matthew, Tell Me about Heaven,* and terminally ill patients express gratitude for the solace it gave them and the people dearest to them. Many write that *Heaven* or *Revelations for a New Era* or *Illuminations for a New Era* answered questions that no other source ever had, and others state that the books' information confirms their deepest feelings. Still others describe their soul-searching and how the books gave them enlightened perspectives of their lives and relationships.

The criteria for selecting representative samples of those kinds of responses [PART II, "Voices of Earth"] included a variety of countries and writers' sentiments and experiences. They aren't meant as "Hurrah for these helpful books," but rather to show how love bonds unite us on Earth and with our dear souls in the spirit world. The same truths are evident in the selection of experiences that the writers (and I) found extraordinary — those are in PART III, "Synchronicity."

As I was reviewing the many e-mails for the few that would get the "divine nudge," I told God that I felt putting any of them in a book was just preaching to the choir. He said the choir needs to know how large it is and that it is continuously gaining new members. *"Sometimes my children feel they are alone with their convictions of what is truth. You can't send each one all the responses you have that are so gratifying to you, but this book can send a few of those as encouragement. That lets the heart feel light, which is the same as love, and that is what this is about."*

When reprints of *Voices* were needed, the original text had to be revised for two reasons. First, three of its short chapters fit well into related information in *Revelations for a New Era* and were included in that book's 2010 revision along with updated information. Second, God wanted changes in *Voices*. He specified what was to be added, wanted updated information where applicable, and deletion of subjects that had widespread interest in 2003, when the book was published, but later waned. All changes in this addition were made in conjunction with the sources of the original material.

It's impossible to know how many people have read the books and Matthew's messages and shared them with others. My gratitude to everyone who has helped to further my mission, "make the information available," is without measure.

Suzanne Ward
February 23, 2011

PART I

VOICES BEYOND EARTH

COMMUNICATION WITH GOD

Hatonn

Suzy: Good morning, Hatonn. I could hardly believe it last night when you said you want to give me a message for "the new book." Didn't you know that I just finished one?

HATONN: Suzy, dear child and friend, yes, of course I know. And you know I'm in charge of communication between Earth and everywhere else, so you know how important this subject is to me. It's been talked about in the other books, but not with the point I wish to make now.

Those whose minds are ahead of their hearts in this matter are unwittingly lagging. The folks who think they have to study this or that to work themselves through their perceived layers of separation from God are just *making* a separation between themselves and God! That is their chosen pathway, so I have no quarrel with it, but it is so *unnecessary!* Especially now, with everything speeding up, they need to know that their spiritual connection with God isn't achieved through mental exercises or incantations or invoking the help of ascended masters—it simply **IS!** Every soul is a part of God, every one **IS** connected with Him! How could it be otherwise when it's the physics of the universe at work here?

This, now, is my presentation, Suzy.

This is Hatonn speaking to you. As master of communication between Earth and the rest of the universe,

I am telling you the simplicity of the answer to your soul-searching: You are a part of God and your connection with Him is your birthright. God IS. You ARE. You and God are ONE. How much more simple can it be? Your soul knows this, and you need only to align your conscious self with your soul, your godself.

You may search through books to learn how to make the communication connection, but those are merely others' ideas of how to reach a stage of spiritual awareness, and that is not necessary. It is as simple as your ASKING! Say, for instance, *"God, I am you, you are me, so please let me hear you."* Or say nothing, just feel it in your heart—God hears that just as clearly. Allow your mind to be still and listen to your soul giving you God's message.

As for searching for God's "will" in your life, as so many of you do, you could say that since you are God in fullness and He is you as a part of Himself, yes, He has a pathway for you. But your own soul as the God part you are *chose* the pathway it needs for growth, and the purpose of your life is to consciously discover that pathway. Conscience is your guide, and so is your intuition. But those can become hidden in the labyrinthine pathway of esoteric studies, lessons, seminars, books—all designed to heighten your awareness of *yet another obstruction* between you and God.

I am not saying for a moment that your studies and sessions are a waste! But how accurately are they assisting you in the direct course to being the gods and goddesses you already ARE? You are yearning to feel something that isn't in books or graphs or seminars. It is the *intimate, personal, private pathway to your godself you need*, not the mysterious mountains and valleys to travel for years and years. Nevertheless, if you have spent years in this journey, start connecting directly with God without further delay!

Think of this: A child comes into an Earth lifetime with knowledge of that direct God connection, that absolute intuitive knowing, that total sensing of inseparability. The child hasn't studied, hasn't spent hours in seminars or been treated to sessions of calling upon help from the ascended masters. The child simply **IS** the godself! Only by orientation *away* from that inner knowing does the passing of your time bring about the separation. Then you search for your connection through those various forms of "how to" reach what *always* has been yours, *always has been* **YOU!**

Suzy, my friend and mutual servant, as we do indeed serve each other, thank you for heeding my call to come to the computer. I'm a soul of few words usually, as you well know, and I have extended myself on this occasion. Sometimes it's necessary to put a hammer to a head to get the attention, so I have done that with this message—it's essential that people know their *constant, direct communication link with God!*

KNOW WHO YOU ARE

God

Suzy: Good afternoon, God.

GOD: My child, yes, it *is* a good afternoon—it's a *fine* afternoon!

The most serious issue facing Earth in this critical time is clear: *Too few of my children know who they are!* A few do, and it is a joy for me to see the light in those who know they are parts of me, who know they are godselves, who know they're an integral part of this universe and inseparable from all other parts. *NOT* knowing this—no, it IS known at soul level, so it's a case of *not remembering*— that's what has allowed everything to come down on my beloved Gaia that you're seeing today.

On one hand, many of my children there think they're the only ones, or at least the only *intelligent* ones, in this universe. On the other hand many write "earth," not even with a capital E to show the same respect given the names of the other planets in your solar system, and there's no name for your moon, but there are names for the moons of other planets as well as for other heavenly bodies. So there seems to be quite a confusion as to the significance you place on your homeland Earth even as you wonder about—or *deny*—other civilizations living "out of sight." I'll come back to that reference in a minute, but I want to continue making my point.

You who believe these other civilizations are "out there" and have given them names—some of which are right, and in any event, identification helps you keep them straight—have labeled some "dark" and others "light." That is fine, too, as far as it goes, designating the "light" ones as benevolent, loving beings—which means love of *self* too!—and in the other fold the dark ones, those that have been manifesting all sorts of horrendous happenings and afflictions in the universe with their free will choices.

Does any of that—the greater or lesser intelligence or the greater or lesser attainment in soul evolution—make any difference to me? Not at all in my love for each life in ANY form—all are parts of me. But those levels of attainment DO make a vast difference in my universe: the knowledge these beings have retained of their beginnings as inseparable parts of me, how they have used their free will, and the extent to which they have developed universal technologies. Some are pure joy to me! Embracing the light gives them knowledge of their godselves and their behavior is in keeping with that.

Others, whom I love equally because they, too, are parts of me, give me heartburn, to use your expression. They started out with light—*every* soul does!—but in their free will, they chose to leave the light—*light is the same as love*—and their choices of behavior dropped accordingly with the lack of light in their souls. Some members of these civilizations have been creating miseries for Earth and her life forms for so long that other civilizations became discouraged.

Yes, *discouraged*—you know this very human feeling!—but never ceasing to love you and root for you to "see the light." In some cases those who became discouraged are your ancestors. They've watched their first generations of Earth humans flourish, then later ones fall because they forgot the knowledge of who they are. Once that happened, the influence of what you call the "dark forces" swooped into souls on Earth and there you have it—the power of the dark in mighty conflict with the power of the light.

And since everything everywhere affects everything else everywhere else, all the realms of civilizations are watching you with keen interest. The discouragement of the "light" beings has turned to rejoicing as they see more of you remembering that you are me, I am you. The forces of the "dark" have revved up to keep those who are still "in the dark" exactly that way. Often you use light and dark expressions—you just don't know their real significance, that light is the same as love and consciously knowing who you are, and dark is the absence of light-love, the absence of that knowing.

You've been led to understand love as something immeasurably less than what it is: **the most powerful force in the universe.** *Nothing* is more powerful than love! Love is the essence of Creator expressed into light energy that vibrates at different frequencies to form the substance of all life in the cosmos, thus in this universe—*love is the material that manifested you!* Sperm uniting with egg is only physical mechanisms at work, but the energy of your very life is love, the original and *only* creational material.

Now then, for untold ages Earth has had this light-dark polarity that just wouldn't stop its jiggling in a tiny spectrum of hidden dark control. Well, now that is stopping, and at this moment, it's nearing the point it must reach so the energy can start swinging back into balance, where all will be well. I'm not giving a scientific explanation here—I'm saying simply that everything in the universe is energy in motion at differing frequencies, and each of you is energy moving at the frequency in accordance with what you think, feel and do. Energy is neutral. It's the power you give it with your attitudes and actions that creates energy's polar attachments of "good" and "bad," for simplest explanation, and it is these extremes that are nearing the opposite ends of the spectrum even as I speak. When they do, the reversal of the intensity of these opposites will begin and LOVE will bring the two sides back into balance wherein light and dark are harmoniously reconciled.

Your world needed a great deal of help to get to this stage of near-polar extremes so the pendulum could start swinging back into balance. My children of light can battle the dark of my flock when attacked themselves, but they cannot interfere with other souls unless they are requested to do so. Earth asked for help to eliminate the control of the dark. She *had* to have help because she had given her light as long as she could, until she was too weakened to continue this by herself. In honoring her request, I gave permission for my parts of light to assist her.

Their help was essential because the long-prevailing corruption, deceit and tyranny of the dark had created fear, hatred, greed, despair, grief, brutality, violence and vengeance all over your planet. The magnified power of those feelings attached itself to energy streamers and formed a layer around Earth to prevent the light from beaming into souls. The reduced light in Earth's souls correspondingly diminished the light of Earth herself.

She is not just a mass in orbit. She is the living composite of every iota of energy within, on and immediately above her, and her soul was in anguish because her planetary body and atmosphere were dying due to the dark grasp on her population that was keeping them from receiving the light. Earth's desire to rid herself of that dark influence led to her cry for help from high light beings—without their help, her body would have perished along with all life forms upon it. Earth needed the light for YOUR survival, for your spiritual clarity and for changing your cellular structure into the crystalline form required for physical survival in the higher vibrations where she is heading. [*Part II, "Universal Energy" in* Revelations for a New Era, *explains this in detail.*]

That is the simple explanation of what is happening on Earth—the light is removing the destructiveness of the dark so your planet can survive. And survive Earth will! The question is: *What will you do?*

That is why this is a critical time on Earth! Those of you who are still "in the dark" need to "see the light" and know who you are! The so-called "dark souls" need to know that they are parts of me with no more and no less importance to me than any others of my children. They need to jump on this bandwagon of self-discovery so they won't get left behind as my precious Earth continues rising into higher vibrations, where the non-discoverers of this universal truth won't have attained the light frequency for physical survival. Their souls will enter realms of energy where their free will choices registered them, and learning—*remembering!*—will begin at rudimentary stages.

Suzy, you've been typing rapidly to keep up with me and there's as much red as black on the screen. Please take a break to correct that and read what I've said.

...... *God, I understand this because of information I received for the books, but I think it's too much to expect people who haven't read them to clearly understand every-thing. Also, it needs to be clarified that good people who are "in the dark" aren't dark souls themselves. Please explain your reference to "out of sight," and I think it's necessary to mention that the energy pendulum isn't going to take "untold ages" to swing back into balance.*

Now maybe you understand why I chose you as my editor! Well, since three books can't be summarized in this one, I suggest that people read those. When we're through talking, please reference all pertinent information in the other books — that's the best we can do for the moment.

But indeed it does need to be clarified that "good people" who are still "in the dark" are *not* the same as dark souls — they've just been kept unaware of the truth by the "authentic" dark souls' teachings that are *intentionally* WRONG! It will be a joy to me when all my children *"see the light"* of my truth, which is in all of these books I've entrusted you to publish. [*As well as describing life in Nirvana, all of* Matthew, Tell Me about Heaven *is about this. Part III "Our Soul Connection" in* Revelations for a New Era *comprehensively covers that aspect of ourselves, and Part III "Talking with God," in* Illuminations for a New Era *gives God's perspective in great detail.*]

Those souls that I said are "out of sight" actually aren't — they're in plain sight, you just don't recognize them. As I've said, Earth's population was started by other civilizations, so it's not new that "aliens" are living there. *Souls* is the important distinction here, not bodies. Souls of many other civilizations are living among you and they look just like you in form and features.

Advanced light beings have the intelligence level to manifest whatever bodies they want, and some have done that on your planet. They can appear as easily as can the records that give them an Earth ancestry. Others are born by natural means, and still others arrive by an agreement between two souls that some call the "walk-in" process.

Dark beings with advanced intelligence also come by natural birth, but only into families of their civilizations, and they also can appear on Earth in manifested bodies of their choice. Others may take over bodies of Earth souls who are having what you call "out-of-body experiences" and these cases sometimes are thought of as someone "being possessed."

Regardless of their origin on Earth, each of these "alien" souls comes for specific purposes. Those of the light come to offer that kind of assistance to all of you who are receptive, and those of the darkness use their influence on you who are weak and willing, like puppeteers pulling the strings of their puppets. This is not easy for you to understand, much less believe, but it is so.

[*The "Soul Transference" chapter of* Revelations for a New Era *explains the "walk-in" process by soul agreement. In that same book, Part IV "Creation" describes the beginning of human life on Earth, and in Part VI "Universal Brotherhood," several representatives of advanced civilizations tell about their ongoing assistance to us.* Illuminations for a New Era *chapter "Reptilian Influence" covers the dark ones of the reptilian civilization, and "possession" is explained in that book's chapter "Astral Travel, Earthbound Souls."*]

As for the pendulum's swing once it reaches its zenith, its journey back to balance will be fast, a matter of a few years, not the near-countless number of years that it has been hovering in the "dark zone." What is transpiring is the *first ever*—never since Creator expressed Itself into angelic love-light and subsequently all other life was initiated in the universes of the cosmos has there been anything like this. Your ideas of time and space don't apply beyond Earth, and there is no way I can explain the reality because within the limitations of the dimension in which you are living, there is nothing which you can relate to the Truth. [*All of the other Matthew Books also give insight insofar as possible, given the limitations of our comprehension and languages.*]

Yes, Suzy, I know all of this will be a jolt to folks who've never heard any of it before, but the reality, which is beyond even imagining there now, will become clearer the farther into the light your civilization ascends.

So then, I believe that's sufficient to explain this critical issue facing Earth, so go ahead and ask the question that has popped into your mind.

Well, I'm just wondering if you ever think about this, that because you always know our thoughts and feelings, we never have any real privacy? There's the energy shield between Nirvana and us that lets our thoughts and feelings be just ours alone when that's what we want. We can simply "shut down," but with you, we can't do that.

My child, do you really want to have to decide with each thought or feeling whether you'd like me to know about it, whether you want my "arms" to guide or enlighten or protect or comfort you? Not that that is even a possibility, but thinking about it will let you feel more comfortable with things the way they are.

You're right. I guess you're always right.

Isn't "right" just like "wrong" — it's a matter of who considers the very same situation to be one or the other?

It seems so.

My beloved child, when you question me, it delights me. It's the blind acceptance of what people are *taught* that they *should believe and feel* that's a problem for me, frankly. Now, would you like to think of another question for me?

Not now, thank you. I think I'll cook dinner.

Bob will appreciate that decision. I'm eager to know what your mind will come up with for us to talk about next.

Well, you'll know before I get to the computer, so you'll be ready for it, whatever it is, won't you?

Yes. Now go, my child, and prepare dinner.

YOU ARE YOUR LIFE'S ARCHITECT

Serapis Bey

Primarily known for his lifetimes in Egypt as a light warrior and an architect pharaoh, Serapis Bey now is among us all etherically. He came from higher realms to be a guardian of Earth's evolution and telepathically has given guidance for souls' disciplined living to aid in their spiritual evolution.

A good day, dear ones, from Serapis Bey, and a very fine day it is! You may associate my name with ancient architecture, and rightly so, yet a builder of much more importance to you than of pyramids and such, ah yes! Most notably in your history as a designer and builder by talent and trade, I shy away from returning in a body for more construction. Instead I am lending my energy, or perhaps "infusing" my energy is more apt, to receptive ones who may or may not realize that their motivation and inspiration are in part in cooperation with me. It does not matter if they do not know. All that matters is that they beautifully express their talents in inspired ways.

But return I do in this manner to whet your appetite to the self-realization and self-actualization of your individual building, *your soul evolution,* by way of LOVE in all undertakings to restore Earth to her former health and beauty. Your homeland is greatly beloved by me and countless others whose great desire never diminished to be of service to her and to all who live upon her.

At one time Earth, when she was known as Gaia or Terra or Shan, was one of the most magnificent of all celestial bodies, a paradise without blemish, and God's favored creation. That was before civilizations came and brought some of their baseness along with their grand intellect. Through the eons since then the degree of intelligence and spirituality of the populations has fluctuated and with that, her well being and pristine beauteousness faded.

During the past many millennia, with the few exceptions of God's chosen messengers and others who also understood their Oneness, the peoples' beginnings were totally lost to memory and they spiraled into an abyss of love-lessness. Love without reservation or condition or expectation; love that acknowledges soul-self's connection with God and all other souls in this universe; love that sees and is thankful for blessings; love, the highest of all vibrations and enables each soul, each god and goddess self, to be a divine powerhouse beyond your wildest imagining, went missing.

Darkness took its place. The absence of that kind of love is why Earth plunged from her high placement in the universe into so-called third density, a thriving hotbed of low vibrations where the basest aspects of what you call "human nature" let havoc abound in every conceivable manner. In other lifetimes, some of you participated in the terrible destructiveness that cost Earth such severe blows that her blood-soaked, light-depleted body was near death and her soul was in deep despair.

Maybe you have memories of those times and know that you returned to mend Earth, to shower your love upon her and ALL her life forms, not only those with special appeal to you, but most of all, those considered despicable, because they are the ones in greatest need of love. Just as

God honored Earth's request for light so she could rise out of the low dimensions and countless members of your family, as yet unknown to you, responded, so do we also honor your souls' requests for light to aid your emergence from non-remembrance into full conscious knowing.

One expression of love is light beams and their healing effects. Therefore, love and light may be used synonymously in language as they are indeed one and the same energy, with only their expressions differing. When there is no light, there is its opposite, darkness, and "darkness" and "dark forces" aptly describe energy streamers carrying dark thought forms that weak persons invite, and those fortify the weak ones' ideas of atrocious motives and actions.

Let me tell you how this happens. You may think that the opposite of love is hatred, but it is not. The opposite of love is its *absence*, a most painful void in the heart space. Into that void can flow the streamer attachments of fear, brutality, greed, deceit and all other manner of low vibrations inherent in base ideas and behavior, but if that void can be filled with love, there is no room for any darkness to enter. When love is in the heart space, no soul is weak.

And love is flowing again in great abundance on Earth! Your love for her—and a most loving, compassionate, nurturing, long-suffering soul she is!—for each other, for all fauna and flora, and for yourselves. Yes, for *yourselves*, and rightly so! How greatly we respect you who asked for and were granted this lifetime to help restore your homeland! Ah, the joy of seeing Earth rejoice as her resident souls fill themselves with love! We yearn for the same in your brothers and sisters who do not remember that they chose to help Earth regain her glory, and thus their own. Yet, we take solace in knowing that if not this time, then at another time they may help some other troubled world rise out of its travails and in so doing, they will rise out of their forgetfulness and know the heights of glory.

And so, beloveds, as architects who step-by-step design and build your destiny on this unique stage of your eternal life, do so with the assurance that I, Serapis Bey, and heavenly hosts without number are with you, adding our light to yours. Keep smiling — ah, the radiance of love in a smile!

For wider availability of the message that Serapis Bey gave me for the book that I contributed to, And Then God Said … Then I Said … Then He Said …, *God wanted it included in this book, and Serapis was delighted.*

BE INFORMED AND *ACT*

God

October 4, 2003

This is a time for rejoicing! The polar extremes in what you call "human nature" have been reached. By universal law, nothing is static for a nanosecond, and the momentum has started to return Earth to the state of balance wherein the extremes will be reconciled. This does not mean perfection — that sublime state exists only within Creator — because your planet will continue to be a learning placement for souls. But the violence, starvation, deception, disease, cruelty — all the devastation caused to Earth and all her life forms by the will of the darkness — will continue to lessen until all are planetary history, and this is to happen during the next several years.

Earth will be restored to her former paradise self as she is rising into higher vibrations — this is *assured!* The critical question still is: *Will you accompany her?* And the answer still is, you will if you have enough light to physically survive in those higher vibrations. *The choice is yours* — that's the good news, and there doesn't have to be any bad news unless you think that absorbing enough light for your personal ascension comes automatically. It doesn't. You have some work to do.

Too many of you still don't see what is so essential — it's going to take some doing on your part to straighten out the mess your world is in. Yes, other civilizations all over "space" are in this with you—you wouldn't be alive there if they weren't—but it is not *their* world, it is YOURS. They can't just pull the strings they know would swiftly return my beloved Gaia to health and rouse all the sleepyheads into remembering who they really are. That isn't their responsibility. It isn't even their prerogative. However benevolent and powerful those light civilizations are, they can only *help* you—they cannot do it all. This is the law of the universe, not an arbitrary cut-off line.

Moreover, what you do affects the entire universe. You are putting out energy with every idea and action, and the motives behind those carry an intensity that most of you don't understand. Energy is neutral in this—it acts only in accordance with what you attach to it, and that is determined by your motives, your intentions. So not only do you have the choice to uplift your home planet or not, you have the choice to do the same for the universe.

Regardless of your individual choices, Earth is going back into the higher vibrations where she was created and her soul never left, just her planetary body spiraled down into the depths of third density, and she would love to have all of you go along with her on her ascension journey. But that decision isn't hers—it's YOURS! She has her free will and *you* have *yours*—it's that simple.

Your free will doesn't come from me, it is *Creator's* gift to all souls. Some have misused this gift, foremost to the detriment of their own soul evolution, but with fallout to billions of other souls whose gift the few are denying the use. I'm not overlooking the fact that karmic experiencing to attain balance is part of what is happening. It is in the myriad cases where this is *not* happening that the situation needs to be remedied, and that is being done by honoring souls' requests for amended pre-birth contracts so they can enter spirit life sooner than they originally chose.

I'm allowed to do that because those requests are *their* soul-level choices, but even though this universe is my domain, I'm bound to honor all of Creator's laws, and usurping or denying the free will of any soul acting with dark intent is against one of those laws. So it's my responsibility to get this situation back on track without doing that and I can't do it without help. Maybe I'd better elucidate a bit here or I'll make myself look like a wimp, which I'm not.

I have explained that I am each of my parts regardless of their spiritual station and as parts of me, all are equally loved even when free will choices are against their own spiritual evolvement because they're interfering with the free will of others. Your religions have defined what "sins" are. Not correctly, though. The ONLY "sin" is interfering with the growth of a soul, whether it is one's own soul or others' souls. Furthermore, "sin" is simply *an error*. It's not what some religious dogmas have judged as evil or as a wrongdoing that can be atoned by performing a prescribed ritual—and certainly not by a sentence of death! If you didn't make errors, you wouldn't be on Earth—you'd be somewhere among the angels or highly spiritually evolved civilizations.

Earth is your schoolhouse—it's one of many, even some you know but don't remember—and it's a good one. The idea is to learn from what you perceive as errors so you can avoid more of the kinds of decisions and actions that are harmful to your soul's growth and often to others' as well. You were given a conscience so you can know when you are aligned with your soul-level contract and when you are straying from it. But a conscience, like anything else that is ignored time and time and time again, goes away as it atrophies from lack of use.

Along with learning from the karmic circumstances you chose to bring balance to your souls' experiencing, you are just as free to make choices that aren't in your soul-level agreements because they're not in your best interests. I cannot impinge upon your individual choices — *nor would I want to!* I just wish you would use your free will wisely. I can't take sides in a great conflict, either, because even though I am *all* of you, I am foremost *EACH* of you. I am as strong as the strongest and as weak as the weakest. As the amalgamation of all my independent yet inseparable parts, I cannot act to change or exclude even one. Balance is what all souls are aiming for because within balance is the spiritual strength of reconciled polarity — that's another of Creator's laws — and I am only as strong as my parts that have achieved this status. So you see, all of my children collectively determine my strength.

There, Suzy, that should take care of explaining why I need help, and now I shall get on with what I have been leading up to. I requested you to state right up front in the last book that these books are not political forums. That still is so, but I cannot ignore this topic of politics because that is what has been running your world — mostly running it into the ground! — almost from the beginning. Not necessarily by that name, but by that ideology, where the strongest few rule over the masses. That can be done wisely, benevolently, with the strong uplifting the weaker to the benefit of all. But instead, what I see is greater and greater political oppression to the detriment of all. The politics that controls all countries, all peoples, all economies and resources of your planet homeland has been instrumental in bringing your world to the devastated state it's in.

In no country on Earth are people free. For millennia the dark souls of civilizations beyond your planet have been influencing their willing Earth brothers and sisters in leadership positions to deceive and intimidate the rest of the people. Almost all in national leadership positions rule by the dictates of those forces that are unknown to the people and perhaps even to the rulers. The influence of those dark alien puppeteers has resulted in all declarations of war and all decisions regarding economies and resources of the world. Their secondary aim is increasing the control and wealth of those whose greed for power makes them eager puppets, thus today you have a world with vast riches in a few hands, impoverished nations, willful environmental destruction and corruption oozing out of corporate connections with governments.

The ultimate aim of the puppeteers is annihilation of your planet. That will NOT happen, but beneficial changes for all require a change in the character of your world's leaders. Voices must be raised with demands for leaders of spiritual integrity—that kind of character is exemplified, not merely proclaimed. I don't mean that no leaders ever have been strong in virtues or that no voices ever have been raised to protest injustice and inequities—indeed there have been those individuals. Many of those brave souls suffered or died for that, and much of their good works has been undone by succeeding generations who blindly followed self-serving leaders.

Now, the collective will of the people is rising to expose and oppose this situation. As lies are exposed, more lies are being told, and those will be exposed too. Tyrannical regimes must and shall change. Although plans are afoot for this peaceful revolution through a joint effort between your civilization and many of your space family, that does not absolve any of you who desire a finer, brighter world from the responsibility of helping to create it. You all chose to be where you are at this time precisely so you could do exactly that! Actually, some of you embodied in other lifetimes as great leaders on Earth and well beyond, and you are back now to take on similar inspirational and constructive roles.

It is on three levels that you must act so that honorable governing bodies will be achieved. The first level is **spiritual**, and I'll tell you what spiritual is NOT: It is not membership in any of the multitude of your religions. It is not the self-righteousness that is evident in great abundance. It is not escaping into a head-in-the-sand "prayer life." It is not believing that neither good nor evil exists because those are only judgments. It is not accepting that every-thing is in divine order and will run its course without your participation. It is not refraining from seeing what is going on in your world because you've been told it's all an illusion anyway. I am not saying that there is no truth in any of that; what I'm saying is that spirituality is not an inherent aspect of any.

The spiritual level on which you will change your leaders from being darkly-ruled themselves to people worthy of being leaders — *true leaders with spiritual integrity* — is within your hearts. That's your usual depiction of where love resides, is it not? Actually, the sensation of love is a province of the soul, but it has strong physical effects at the heart that instantly spread throughout your entirety to uplift you in spirit, mind and body.

Love starts with self, with living so that loving self is as natural as breathing. Only then can you give and receive love. Love is contagious, unlimited, omnipresent. It is what changes bleakness of spirit into fullness of spirit, illness into health, lack into prosperity. It is the *absence of love* that breeds all the woes of your world, and it is filling the void with love that will cure the woes. This is not asking you to love what brings misery and deprivation and harm! It is asking you to simply *feel* love so you can send forth that energy — it will seek its way to the void.

The second level is **mental** — deeply thinking to discern what is truth and what isn't instead of buying into what candidates say. The catch is, what information is truthful and what is not? What sources can be trusted? You have been deceived for eons by a few souls in one generation after another after another whose intent is to retain the control over you, so access to the truth is not easily come by. How can I put this so it is not a series of Don'ts? Always I prefer to be positive in statements, and I've already compromised that by my explaining what being spiritual *isn't*.

Very well, I know how to proceed — think of what you *want* in your world. If that is peace and harmony and cooperation, that's where to focus your thoughts. What will bring that to the world? Think of what will: Respect and dignity for all races and faiths and genders; help wherever help is needed; equitable sharing of Earth's massive riches; cures of all diseases; education, fulfilling work and comfortable homes for everyone; honesty, kindness, compassion, fairness, harmony, sharing, justness, forgiveness.

Think of all those qualities and circumstances and let your heart and conscience guide you to the candidates you most closely identify with them. The words of campaign promises are worthless without a candidate's heart and soul in them. Let *your* heart and soul, not just your eyes and ears, lead you to the persons who exemplify the love and light that's needed to uplift your world.

The third level is **action**. If you want leaders whom you trust and respect, work toward that end. Publicly and financially support the people you want in office, but if that isn't possible, then put forth your intention through the power of your energy focused on those persons *actually holding the positions*—I can't emphasize too strongly the power of *intent!* You can be sure that the current people in power will have their supporters actively working because those folks get the trickle-down largesse in exchange. You who want love, peace and harmony will receive those incomparably greater victories in exchange for the energy you put forth to create them.

Because that grand and beautiful country called America is pivotal in determining what happens all over the planet, its presidential election is of international interest. However, the three levels of involvement I have just delineated apply to *all* people in the world as they pertain to this upcoming election. Discernment of information and energy are without national boundaries or distance limitations, so a person in South Africa or Brazil or China or Egypt or Australia has the same power of focusing intent as any USA citizen.

Yes, of course that applies to every person in every country and their own leaders. However, most corrupt governments are obvious and the United States supposedly is a haven for democracy, but that is a farce of the highest order. You may believe that legal and honest processes are observed in "democratic" elections there, but it has been many, many decades since the last of those. There haven't been any honest elections anywhere else on Earth, either, but it's not as apparent that there haven't been any in the United States, where the citizens have been duped for such a long time into believing their voices and votes count.

The men and women in the federal government are not

ruling that country "with freedom and justice for all." Those are hollow words, just as the two-party system is meaningless insofar as giving voters a choice—the dark forces have influence that knows no party lines. Government officials who have acted in accordance with their sense of honesty and right-ness have been disposed of by one means or another. Those who are not killed are threatened with it or they are ridiculed into non-credibility or are forced out of influence into oblivion. That is what has been passing as the "democratic system of government" in America.

Only with an honest voting process can the people's choices be given their true value, and you citizens of USA don't have that. Your votes are denied, ignored or manipulated to serve the interests of the "power elite," one term used to denote the few most powerful people on Earth who are controlling everything everywhere to serve themselves. If you want to have an honest election for a change, work toward that end. Investigate the voter eligibility rolls and balloting mechanisms, the people who handle the ballots, the company that counts them and releases the totals to the media for announcing. I tell you, there is deception and corruption up and down the line, and curing that ill has to precede the next presidential election or it will be business as usual.

Do I endorse a candidate? No, and telling you my choice isn't what this is about. I am ALL of the candidates, remember, and I'm not about to tell you which is YOUR choice. It's *your* free will decision that counts, but first you need to get an honest balloting system in place, which is NOT the case now, or your vote won't be worth a fig.

That's it, Suzy. What do you think of that for a nonpolitical message?

I like it because I see my choice for president fitting in there exactly. I hoped you'd name him even though I didn't really expect that. But would you comment on him, please?

He's the one with the most light.

Isn't that the same as he would be the best president?

It's more. He would be in the position to lead the reforms your whole world needs and he is the one who can do that. Let's talk about something else.

OK, how about NESARA? [National Economic Security and Reformation Act]

My dear, I can't do any better than what Matthew has told you. Please add that as a chapter and then let's call it a day.

February 1, 2011

Hi, God, are you busy?

What would you say if I told you I've run out of things to do?

Probably laugh – well, I just did. You gave me that message over seven years ago and there have been two US presidential elections since then, so don't you want to delete the obsolete part about the US election?

Suzy, how can explaining the way to get people with spiritual and moral integrity into leadership positions be obsolete when elections there still are in the hands of a powerful few? And not just in your country, but in many, and there still are dictators that need to be ousted. Furthermore, what I said in that message is an accurate part of your country's history — a lot of what's in the history books isn't anywhere near what actually took place.

Well, what about your grim picture of elections here — didn't that change when Obama became president?

Oh come, come, Suzy! You know he's a major player in the Golden Age master plan and nothing could have prevented his election.

Well, yes, but still it's rather surprising that the Illuminati's usual tactics to put in office whomever they want didn't work.

Oh, they fully intended his opponent to win, and according to the announced vote count it looked like a reasonably close race, but the actual votes cast for Obama were in such overwhelming numbers that they had to declare him the winner or there would have been a real hullabaloo. Matthew could have told you that if you'd thought to ask him.

I didn't — as you know! What about the elections that aren't part of that master plan?

The Electoral College and state districting favor the elite powerhouse, which is their intention, and so do long-timer incumbents' political "machines." But after that fiasco in Florida with those dangling chads and the Supreme Court deciding that the president would not be the people's choice, the election process has been cleaned up a bit, but not enough to deserve being called "democratic" by a long shot.

You know I'm not really into politics, that my interest is getting the reforms our whole world needs, and that's what else I want to ask you – what's your opinion on how those are coming along?

If my umbrella self, as you usually think of me, could step in, things would be moving a lot faster and you would have seen results long before now, but you know that I have to bide my time just like you do. The really big changes are still brewing, waiting for exposure of the really big lies that have been molding life on Earth for so long. In the messages you distribute, Matthew has talked about the heavy guns opposing everything your president is there to do not just for his country but for the world, so I'm not going to repeat that.

Give me a minute here. Suzy, what Matthew has said about Barack Obama and the master plan of the Golden Age is a part of Earth's history that must be included in this book—it's the only way that collection of important information can be preserved in one record. Hatonn chimed in on that too, so please add what he said. Put it all in a separate chapter, title it Barack Obama and place it after the one where Matthew talks about the Illuminati—people need to know who they are so they can understand what Obama is up against. End this first part of the book with Matthew's explanation of NESARA and add Hatonn's later messages. People need to know that this currently terribly misunderstood program is the legal groundwork of the Golden Age master plan.

OK, God. So, how much darkness still has to be eliminated?

ALL of it, Suzy! But I know what you mean, how much is left to deal with. Only a smidgen compared with the light there, but a few power-mongers still are running parts of the show, like digging in their heels to keep a tight lid on those big lies I mentioned. And they still have enough control so that my children in other civilizations who have been waiting patiently—well, *mostly* patiently—to land and help you get rid of pollution and so forth instead are still flying around in circles above you. They can't join you on the ground until there's certain safety for everyone and at this point, it's still too risky to officially acknowledge their existence. But things are heating up so that can't be delayed much longer.

God, we've heard that for 20 years or more and we're getting tired of waiting.

My sweet child, who knows that better than I? I am the *collective* tiredness of everyone who feels like that. I also am the *collective excitement* in anticipating that day when you'll greet members of your universal family!

Little Suzy, I've given you a big chore, locating all those message parts to put in the next chapter. I'll be working with you and we'd better hop to it.

THE ILLUMINATI

Matthew

The Illuminati's corruption and deception are being exposed by defectors, witnesses, interested researchers and investigative reporters, but that powerful group is fighting tenaciously to keep their control over governments, the global economy, Earth's natural resources and everything else that impacts life in your world. The light forces have been just as tenacious in efforts to eliminate that control, which is why formerly hidden situations are "coming to light" and there is such turmoil in Earth's energy field of potential.

Evidence that their power is waning is, despite their control over what is reported in your mainstream media— which are owned by a few Illuminati—those "news" outlets now are reporting what the light has exposed. To have any credibility whatsoever, they no longer can withhold information that only a few years ago would not have seen the light of day by that means. Certainly not all the truth is being reported, nor is everything that is reported true, but the Illuminati stronghold on you via the media is cracking.

They gave themselves that name, which means "the enlightened," but they don't publicly refer to themselves as Illuminati. They work in secret but the results of their activities are seen throughout your world. Their members are in governments and regulatory bodies; agencies dealing with national and international economies and banking; royal families; international corporations; the United

Nations; law, policing and justice systems; educational institutions; media and entertainment venues; church hierarchies; the Zionist movement; multinational corporations. Probably I forgot some groups and organizations under the Illuminati umbrella, but in short, they influence everything that affects life in your world.

On Earth they are the people whose greed and control went way beyond their soul-level agreements, which was to serve in powerful positions to balance their own karma and a multitude of others' chosen karmic experiencing. At the point when the collective karma had been completed, the intensity of greed and control in the Illuminati members was to have quickly reversed into the equitable sharing of their resources and power. However, with full knowing of their soul-level agreements and the consequences of not abiding by those, the most powerful members of this group refused to honor their agreements. These hard-core few kept on amassing the planet's resources, oppressing the peoples, and creating divisiveness and conflict.

They have been told that they will not be able to continue doing that, but they are deaf and blind to all urgings of the light, and in their intention to relinquish nothing, they are using every possible means to keep lower-level members of the group fighting for this as well. Some defectors who turned to the light in accordance with their soul contracts have been assassinated, and family members have been killed as a warning to those in influential positions where the peak Illuminati want to maintain control. In the more weak-willed members, bribery is successful because greed is in the hearts of all Illuminati, and threats of exposing embarrassing information about personal lives is another common means to keep those folks toeing the line.

Now, above the Earth human Illuminati top level are the dark souls of the reptilian civilization, some of whom are embodied as humans and living on the planet. They are working in conjunction with their dark colleagues off-planet, whose goal is total domination of Earth, if not by absolute control, then absolute destruction. The light forces of the universe—and that includes light-filled reptilians—are in confrontation with the darkness of any and all civilizations. What is happening on your planet is a reflection of the universal conflict, and regardless of how things go on the other battlefronts, *Earth will be freed from the clutches of darkness and ascend into the vibratory plane where love and peace prevail!*

BARACK OBAMA

Excerpts of Matthew's and Hatonn's messages:

May 21, 2008   Attention is being given around the globe to the United States presidential candidates. Despite the rigged primary elections to favor Hillary Clinton and John McCain's supporters waffling because he himself waffles, soon it will be glaringly apparent that Barack Obama's greater popularity among voters will be sustained. Thus free will choices of the majority have been made and now, without influencing those choices one whit, we can reveal that in the energy field of potential, Obama's momentum always was unstoppable, and we can tell you that this highly evolved soul with many lifetimes as a wise and just leader came from a spiritually and intellectually advanced civilization specifically to rise to his current prominence.

At soul level he knows this is his mission, but consciously he is aware only of his innate leadership abilities and genuine intent to serve his nation as he so states; in time he will become consciously aware of his origin and purpose for embodying in this lifetime. Once he is in office, some darkly-intentioned persons expect to control him just as they and others before them have controlled a succession of US presidents and many members of Congress. However, that vicious kind of governing is at an end, and contrary to the protestations of Hillary Clinton that this race is not over, she and other top Illuminati know they are

witnessing the demise of their "secret government"; therefore, the Obama family members are among the most
intensely light-protected persons on Earth.

July 4, 2008   We see presidential nominee Barack
Obama's supporters' uneasiness about his recent statements
and decisions that are disappointing and seem to contradict
his previous stance. Because the next US president issue is
of international interest and his momentum toward office
is unstoppable, we hasten to assure that he is doing only
what he must to ostensibly align himself with the expectations of the Illuminati.

Although their power base is in tatters, they still have
enough punch to sway election results by fraudulent vote
count, bribery and life threats to families of anyone who
opposes them. So do be at peace if the "public" Obama has
become worrisome to you—it is like many other situations
that are not what they appear to be and time will so tell. We
can say this without jeopardizing his and his family's
physical safety—not only are they surrounded by light
warrior protectors, but who among potential assassins
would give credence to what the "voice in her head" says?

July 27, 2008   How can I say Barack Obama is a light
being? Because he is. For the benefit of new readers, I shall
paraphrase what I said about him in prior messages, starting
with his unstoppable momentum toward the presidency.
At this point, he is only following a strong sense of urgency
to lead his country out of its downward spiral and his
conviction that he can do this, but in time he will be
consciously aware that he is a soul from an intellectually
and spiritually advanced civilization and embodied on
Earth specifically to fulfill this mission. What he has been

very clear about all along is that he must appear to be aligned with the Illuminati goals; otherwise, he never could have become the Democratic party nominee. This accounts for his veering on some issues that have disappointed some of his supporters, who have no idea that what he is doing is in accordance with Illuminati "guidance." Time will show that his essence, intentions and actions are aligned with the light.

November 21, 2008   How could we know this [presidential election] outcome even before votes were cast in the primary election? We knew of this highly evolved soul's destiny before he was born because it is in the continuum, where there is no linear time and all potential exists, like raw clay for a sculptor. Just as the sculptor labors to produce the object of his vision, so does all directed energy turn any potential into the actuality of the vision.

Your recorded history is but a minute fraction—and a very inaccurate fraction at that—of your planet's universal history, which is accurately known in the continuum. For millennia darkness controlled the minds and hearts of the peoples, and lifetime after lifetime souls incarnated with the self-chosen mission to break free of that control, yet all except a very few continued to fail. They were not bereft of the self-empowerment every being has as a god or goddess self; it is that the fear perpetrated and perpetuated by off-planet dark forces and implemented by its puppets on the planet was so pervasive that knowledge at soul level was blocked from reaching consciousness.

All the while, the light that was Earth's very life force became dimmer and dimmer. In conjunction with her choice to ascend out of the depths of third density, where her planetary body no longer could survive the ever accumulating negativity, the alignment of celestial bodies and the strategic direction of energy presented another opportunity for light to vanquish the darkness that so long had controlled life on the planet. This time history would not be repeated. This time there would be the assistance Earth needed and requested, a massive infusion of light from other civilizations that not only would assure her survival as a planet, but also would enlighten her residents so they could make conscious choices in keeping with Earth's vision of a peaceful, healthy world where humankind lives in harmony with Nature.

Only in the timelessness of the continuum could the countless complexities needed to manifest that vision into reality be most carefully considered and arranged. A foremost consideration was the cosmic law, that Creator's gift of free will with its inseparable power of manifestation had to be honored; and because the world Earth desired would be co-created for and BY her residents, it would have to be according to what they envisioned. Each individual manifests his or her personal life and, in combination, all the lives make up the world; so it was necessary to insure that enough of the collective minds would be enlightened, inspired and dedicated to creating the Golden Age of Earth's vision. Of paramount importance was the balance that had to be achieved through completion of the third density karma that had been incurred by souls in their multiple lifetimes on Earth and various other places in the universe. And there was the need for souls to come from highly spiritually and intellectually evolved civilizations to be the way-showers and leaders of the souls who were less evolved.

Carrying out the mandate of God, who was honoring Earth's free will to ascend, members of galactic and intergalactic federations sought counsel of the highest beings in this universe, and out of discussions at that level, a plan was developed that would enable Earth to leave third density, where darkness thrives, and rise into fifth density, where darkness cannot exist. During her ascension process, third density karma would have to be played out, so most roles were for very difficult experiences: impoverishment or brutally oppressive regimes; lives cut short by war, genocide, starvation, murder; grief; physical or mental debilities or incapacitation; slavery, legal injustice; family, national and international discord — everything that could assail body, mind and spirit had to be over and done with. Some souls had to be the individuals who would cause all the suffering, hardships, disharmony and death so the masses could complete their unfinished karmic experiencing.

Knowing all the ramifications of the plan, and because unconditional love for all souls is the basis for each choosing its role in the lifetimes it affects, many more souls than could inhabit the planet during the ascension decades wanted to participate. Those who were not selected to embody would contribute in other vital ways, and those who were selected looked forward to filling the roles that would let them evolve themselves at the same time they were assisting others in their spiritual growth.

Thus, regardless of celestial origin and current culture, age, skin color, religion, gender, ethnicity, or nation of residency, *prior to birth* all peoples now on the planet knew the soul who would incarnate as Barack Obama and joyfully agreed to his becoming president of the United States to lead that country and the world into the Golden Age. All participant souls were born with that knowledge, but it was forgotten in the adjustment to "life in the flesh" and its needs, and even more so, indoctrination by family, educators, religion and society. But they all knew that would happen because it is inherent in third density embodiment; therefore, according to the plan, light in ever increasing intensity has been provided by beings throughout the universe to merge Earth peoples' consciousness with their soul level knowingness.

So, what is considered in your world to be a recent political event had its beginnings long ago in your counting of time and is far, FAR more than Obama's imminent presidency! Think of the innumerable times "historic" has been used to describe this, and rightly so! However, most people have no idea how truly historic it is—they have not yet reached their soul's knowledge that includes what I just explained or what I and other sources of messages have told you through our receivers: *This era on Earth is unique, what is happening is unprecedented in the universe.*

Now then, some "down-to-Earth" issues. First, the expressed concerns about the individuals Obama has met with or appointed. Not only must he ease out of toeing the line set by those who thrust him into the limelight—most of them are following through with their own pre-birth agreements—but he has no presidential authority yet to initiate dramatic changes, and actions within his current range of decision-making are not cast in stone. Replace your concerns about his safety with gratitude for the shield of protective Christed light surrounding him, and yes, the light in your prayers does indeed add to his well being. We encourage you to be patient while everything unfolds, knowing without any doubt whatsoever that the light is in control!

March 10, 2009   Because US President Obama is a major factor in the master plan, let us speak about him.

Some see his administration moving boldly in new directions, others see it following the same policies as the former administration, and still others see it acting on too many fronts without well-defined objectives. To all who regard with pessimism the decisions and actions thus far, we say: *Wait and see!* Despite the formidable situations Obama inherited and the determined opposition of Illuminati members of Congress and those who are acting under that dark group's influence, whether by bribery, blackmail or death threats to family, he will pursue his visionary course to benefit his nation and the world.

May 26, 2009 Moving on to another topic in many minds, that US President Obama's recent decisions are discouraging, just "more of the same." Please remember how often my messages have stated that we are apolitical, impartial and nonjudgmental, that we only report what we observe from our vantage point and information from our many light sources. It is on that basis that I say, the person who wrote that Obama is being "micro-criticized" termed it appropriately.

While some steps in the direction he intends to lead are receiving the congressional support he requires, opposition to major changes still is fervent because Illuminati pressure upon members of Congress still is fierce. It is the same with that country's military forces and the international industrial, banking and commerce complexes. Obama cannot be, nor does he wish to be a dictator, and he inherited a global bag of worms, so to say. What has been called his "flip-flopping" actually is careful and wise maneuvering as he becomes aware of more elements in the insidious web the Illuminati has tightly woven around the globe. Efforts underway — some are "transparent," but of necessity, many more are progressing behind closed doors—will lead to exposure and riddance of the dark influence that has set the direction of many previous administrations and is trying to do the same in the current administration.

June 24, 2009 Certainly the highly evolved soul that Obama is does not need our defense, and that is not what we are doing by explaining what he is dealing with. Our purpose in speaking of this is to state that not only is an individual's balance disturbed by the energy of distress—or discontentment, disappointment, disillusionment, anger—but also that energy goes forth and adds to the negativity Earth has to transmute into light. Thus, far better than feeling negative emotions about what Obama *appears* to be doing is staying positively focused on the world as you want it to be.

So then, what is he dealing with? In short, the incremental dismantling of the Illuminati worldwide network. As background on this pernicious "umbrella group," only the topmost members know the full extent of its infiltration into governments, banking, commerce, religions, education, media, science, entertainment—all bodies that most impact life in your world. Below those few peak individuals are the ones who control the many facets of the global network. Each has general knowledge about the others but no detailed information about any operations except what he or she is in charge of. The farther down the hierarchy a member is, the more secrecy enshrouds the reasons for the Illuminati's very existence; and at the bottom are the many thousands who simply follow instructions without a glimmer of understanding what real purpose they are serving, somewhat like a 1000-

piece jigsaw puzzle dumped out of the box—no piece is aware of the interconnectedness of all the pieces, much less suspect that altogether they form a whole picture. In the case of the Illuminati, that picture is sinister indeed.

After assuming office, President Obama was briefed on information he had no way of knowing prior to that time, and to continue our analogy, each of the briefers had only a few puzzle pieces. Furthermore, Obama was faced with a dire global economic situation that purportedly started with "toxic" mortgages in the United States, and he needed a knowledgeable, experienced team who could take immediate steps to prevent worldwide collapse. The enormity of the Illuminati's economic network is known in fullness only by the peak of that group, but by connecting puzzle pieces, Obama has become aware of that entanglement and the fortunes hidden in off-shore banks, but the total picture puzzle that will show how that money has been used to manipulate and dominate the world's peoples has yet to be put together.

As difficult as it is to imagine the extent of organizational complexity that is the Illuminati's base of power and influence, it is even more difficult to totally eliminate it. Discovery and legal means to rid the world of that insidious control are underway, and until all is in readiness, it would be foolhardy to make public those efforts. Thus neither the Illuminati nor the Obama camp want their respective activities to become public knowledge, and the "transparency" he promised in good faith must for a while longer be "behind closed doors" instead. As the light continues steadily intensifying and truths no longer can be hidden or denied, you will see the results of his wise course that in this moment seems to belie many of his campaign promises.

December 17, 2009 From his beginning days in office, Obama has been confronted with powerful opposition to his godly vision for his country and a world at peace, and while never wavering one iota from his ultimate intentions, he has had to make compromises and interim decisions that are not in consonance with his vision, with messages from his soul. Ironically perhaps, the same energies that are inspiring gifts from the heart on an unprecedented scale also are causing those who are against all reforms to dig in their heels more stubbornly than ever; through bribery, blackmail or life-threats, the individuals who have woven the pernicious web of darkness still are calling many political shots. Obama and the members of Congress who share his vision will tenaciously pursue the liberation of their government from those self-serving ones who wish to keep it under their control.

This is not unique to the United States, it is happening in countries throughout your world. What is occurring behind the scenes within and among governments will result in triumph for all light-filled peoples, and the dark ones in ruling bodies and every other organization that impacts life on Earth will disappear. As planetary vibrations continue to rise, those ruthless manipulators will leave; their physical bodies cannot survive without the light that they refuse to accept, and the souls will go to worlds that correspond to their lifetime energy registration.

October 10, 2010 — *Hatonn* Generally speaking, people know US president Barack Obama only by what he says and what your media report. Most don't have a clue about what goes on "behind closed doors." You see stubborn partisan politics. We see Obama's powerful enemies within and far beyond the government who are determined to smash to smithereens his attempts at reform. You see him looking worried and know some call him weak and say he's leading his country in the wrong direction. We feel his pain as his efforts to improve the lives of all who are downtrodden are scuttled by a few self-servers. You see him trying to end foreign conflicts and think he should stay home and fix what's wrong in his own country. We feel his discouragement and exhaustion as the dark ones keep stirring up trouble to dash his efforts *everywhere.*

The folks you call "pundits" speculate whether voters will give Obama a second term in office. We sing his praises for staying the course day after day! He has to deal with some of the very ones who threaten his life and his family's, yet his intention to keep working for a peaceful world without poverty anywhere remains firm. *You* know that he and his family are protected by the Christed light grid around them, but Obama doesn't know that. *You* know that he is a major part of the Golden Age master plan, but he doesn't know that either. He acts on his convictions, principles, aspirations and innate experience as an honored leader in a highly evolved civilization who agreed to serve Earth in the most demanding position on the planet. If everyone could know this soul as we do, all the doubts and carping about him would come to a screeching halt and you would thank God for this man's courage, wisdom, spiritual and moral integrity and his willingness to persevere!

You know that your thoughts create what happens in your life, in your world, and everything you do affects everything else in this universe. So if any of you are among the carpers and doubters, stop that and start helping Obama to succeed! He's working *for* you — *do the same for him, yourselves, your world and our universe!* You don't have to become political activists. Just keep your hearts and minds in the right place and help others do it too. We're in the trenches *with you* and we need your help—we have more than enough hindrance from the dark ones on Earth!

I know I've sounded harsh, but sometimes people don't respond until it's "tough love" time, and it *is* with love for you that I've spoken. And not just for myself and my people. I'm representing countless others who feel the same but don't have a forum like this to express it.

NESARA

Matthew and Hatonn

August 7, 2003

My greetings in love to all! This is Matthew. I have requested my mother to receive this important message and pass on to her usual sources for disseminating. I believe that my credibility as one of God's messengers has been established with those who are familiar with the Matthew Books and my messages that have been posted on various Internet sites. In any event, I have been appointed by the highest light beings to speak more comprehensively than I have previously about the vital Earth reformation program commonly known as NESARA. [*National Economic Security and Reformation Act.*] Before that, I say this: NESARA *WILL be implemented*, and it will be done more quickly if its reality is trusted and all who know of it hold convictions toward that success!

Some consider NESARA to be political and economic in nature while others view it as spiritual because of the high level light beings affiliated with it. NESARA is both. When people are severely oppressed by political and economic conditions that foster impoverished living circumstances, lack of health care and education, monopoly of natural resources, slave labor, unjust laws and courts, starvation, and tyrannical regimes, offering "soul food" isn't enough. When people are preoccupied with mere

survival requirements, giving them only spiritual
messages is not going to bring about the global reforms
they need to rise out of their misery. That is why the
provisions of NESARA are monumental in scope,
embodying sweeping reforms for Earth that will begin as
soon as the legislation is officially announced. When
people become aware of the reforms, they will be motivated
to participate according to their capabilities.

As in all other aspects of polarity still existing on Earth,
NESARA is at one extreme and the dark forces that Dove
and the members themselves call the Illuminati are at the
other. Mother, I need to interject something here. The work
Dove is doing to inform about the progress of NESARA is
imperative, and it is essential that her credibility and value
be understood on Earth just as it is in the higher planes,
where it is given great honor.

Now I return to explaining the darkness of the
Illuminati. This powerful cabal has long recognized that to
retain their control of Earth's people, they must keep them
in ignorance and fear, and for millennia that has worked
well for those currently in power and their long line of dark
predecessors. Now they are realizing that it cannot work
for them much longer, and they are sparing no tactic to
hold onto their fast-ebbing control. They rightly see
NESARA as their total uprooting, because once the
program's reforms are implemented, the control of the
darkness will crumble totally.

It is necessary that you understand the reality that is
beyond the religious and scientific dogma that have
structured, dominated and limited your awareness.
NESARA is far more than a piece of legislation in the
United States. The extraterrestrial beings at high stations of
soul evolvement who initiated the ideas within NESARA's

programs to assist Earth humans' rise in spiritual clarity are doing so at the invitation — indeed, the *plea!* — of Earth. Your planet could have not survived any more assaults of the negativity being continuously generated by human brutality to each other, to the animal and plant kingdoms or to the physical body of Earth. All wars and other violence, famine, disease, ruthless leaders, environmental destruction and economic strangulation have been instituted by the influence of the dark forces.

Relief from all the suffering caused by these conditions was essential or your planet would die. Over half a century back in your counting, Earth had reached that point of damage to her body and soul. She had the choice of allowing her planetary body to die or survive intact. Her soul chose the survival of the planet, but in its greatly weakened condition due to the extent of trauma Earth had long suffered, she could not do it without massive assistance. Light beings of extraterrestrial civilizations responded to her cry for help, and among these countless souls who have come to her rescue are those who have been working with diligence and dedication to the reforms embodied in NESARA. So you see, it is by Earth's quest for help that these beings, in conjunction with Earth humans, are performing their various missions on and off-planet to get this vast, vital program underway to rejuvenate physical Earth and enlighten and uplift her people.

It is understandable that you who are familiar with Dove's reports could become discouraged by the delays in NESARA's announcement because you have no "behind the scenes" knowledge of what is causing these. There are two major reasons. First, the NESARA legislation is being processed within the laws of the God-inspired original US constitution. It is important that you understand this is *not* a take-over by ETs to initiate the light in these programs, however desperately needed by Earth. In *collaboration* with wise, just and highly spiritual Earth humans, ETs are helping in myriad ways to restore health to your planet. Knowing of Earth's travail and out of their love for her, spiritually advanced souls chose to reincarnate as Earth humans and assist their universal brotherhood in recreating heaven on Earth, and some are doing this through NESARA's provisions.

Second, the dark forces are fighting tooth and nail to prevent even the awareness of NESARA, much less its implementation, and at this point, delaying the announcement that must by law precede enactment of the widespread provisions is the only weapon left to them. They have been successful thus far in achieving delays by many means: assassinations of influential people who favor initiating the provisions without delay as well as others actively working toward this end; death threats to the families of lightworkers and to the workers themselves; double-agents within the ranks of the lightworkers; and terrorist assaults. The US internal terrorist act of September 11, 2001, was the most dramatic of these tactics. The laboratory-produced SARS disease was meant to be another global fear instigator, but its effects were greatly reduced by lightworkers on and off-planet.

Another delaying tactic is disinformation and non-information through control of major media. The disinformation program includes claims that NESARA as reported by Dove and she herself are frauds. Dove has reported information accurately as it has been given to her, and it has been discouraging to her, not only to you readers of her reports, that time after time the announcement has been delayed. In the beginning of spreading the word about NESARA, it was necessary to get your attention, to encourage you to generate positive energy attachments to the program and give it impetus, and that is achieved by the power of your thoughts and feelings. I cannot emphasize too strongly that your active participation in adding to the light energy momentum is *essential* — NESARA is to *your* benefit! However, since nothing in the universe is isolated in its effects on everything else, it is within universal interests that Earth be lifted out of the third density limitations that for eons have kept you from knowing your eternal and inseparable connection with All That Is. NESARA is an integral part of this planetary ascension into higher vibratory dimensions.

Additionally, it is not correct to believe that even at this high station we can make accurate predictions in the linear time that exists on Earth and nowhere else in the universe. We can look into the energy field of potential and see the increased momentum of the light progress, which at that moment is optimistic and is reported as such. Then the dark forces strike again, and that optimism is tempered by the energy momentum they have gained.

When my mother first was asked for my viewpoint on NESARA, over a year and a half past in Earth counting, I confirmed its validity and the great benefits of its provisions, and I said that their implementation was not imminent. There was limited action in the field of potential then, and nothing registered there indicated that sufficient energy was being generated by the combined on and off-planet light forces so that NESARA would be announced any time "soon."

Two factors were — *are* — affecting NESARA as in everything else: A great deal of planetary and individual karmic balancing still had to be played out, and by Creator's law, souls' free will must be respected except in the case of nuclear detonations in space. That includes the free will choices made by members of the dark forces to hold up and weaken — preferably *doom* — NESARA. Both Earth humans and extraterrestrials among you who look just like you have been using one tactic after another to delay NESARA's announcement. Please don't be disturbed by the fact that darkly-inclined extraterrestrials are operating on Earth — even more powerful extraterrestrial light beings also are among you. The dark ET's, through inculcating in you greed, hatred, violence, ignorance and fear, want to continue to control you and your planet. The light ETs are there *to help you take back control of your planet and your lives!*

Whereas a year and a half ago there was limited energy being registered in the field of potential, now it is in total frenzy. This reflects the extent of energy being generated by the light beings to dislodge the darkness and those forces' last ditch efforts to hang onto their pockets of power that will be lost with the global changes NESARA will usher in. So, while you now can see why the date of NESARA's announcement cannot be estimated with accuracy, you can see that the time is coming closer with each passing day.

Light is the tangible, directional facet of love, and love is the most powerful energy in the universe, the original creating material. NESARA is created in light-love. Do not doubt its power to transform Earth into the paradise it once was. Your part in this transformation is to let this truth of NESARA be known and to trust in its glorious intent and outcome!

With divine grace and the love of the universe, this is Matthew.

[*During the two years following Matthew's explanation of NESARA, its announcement was repeatedly prevented by the Illuminati. To keep to Earth's ascension timetable, NESARA's leadership had to stop their announcement attempts and take a new direction to achieve the same goals. A great deal of false information and confusion ensued: Dove chose to continue in NESARA's former direction, then asked for capital investors to join her; to deny the real NESARA, a US government site was developed and called the National Economic Stabilization and Recovery Act; some channels were distributing messages from low entities who claimed they were Hatonn and other respected light sources, and those entities gave other kinds of disinformation about NESARA; and lightworkers didn't know what to believe. All of that is why Hatonn asked me to receive the following messages.*]

July 18, 2005 I'd like to lay to rest this NESARA announcement business for once and for all. Getting to the point of proving that NESARA is real is an ongoing process with a great deal of progressive activity that has not been given to any channel. Any and all messages that have been giving dates and telling of hostages and CNN takeovers — and especially the *killings!* — are NOT coming from any of us! I assure you, nothing I've ever said to any channel has been in that realm of the absurdity!

That leaves the DISinformation specialists in either spirit or in body as the "newsmakers." What's to be accomplished besides confusion and disillusionment in the believers and jeers from the crowd that always has doubted there is a NESARA? Isn't that enough mischief? From our viewpoint, it is! The energy wasted in both camps is distressing! I'm in charge of all communication between

Earth and all points elsewhere, and there's this hodgepodge of false information going around that I'm trying to get straightened out! I wish the well-meaning people who are sending around those messages with such elaborate explanations would stop and think, *"Would 'ETs' and Sananda really send us all those details?"* They would see how unlikely that is and look elsewhere for verification of true happenings. I strongly suggest they look to their godselves, where *all* truth is known!

By the day we near the time when NESARA will be known—no, I didn't say "announced" because I don't mean announced, I mean *known*—but we don't know when that day will be. We aren't sitting idly waiting for it to amble into sight—we're doing everything within the processes that govern any US legislation so that never can they throw at us, *"You took over our planet!"* Of course this is bigger than the US president and his administration's power group, but they always have the ear of the rest of the world.

Those of you who are familiar with Matthew's messages know that he has made the point several times that even without NESARA's announcement, forward movement is constantly underway toward the same goals. That is exactly what is going on—we're progressing on the same fronts by other means. Anything we do is not by our decision alone, but in conjunction with your own people who will emerge as the vanguard of the transitional government.

There are two ways this can go. Nothing is written in stone and we don't know which way at this point will best serve you. Things can be changed by going what you'd call forward or backward in time. We don't expect you to understand this, so you simply have to trust that we're proceeding cautiously and wisely so that the logistics of major changes will come about as smoothly as possible. This isn't a revolution in the sense that your history books tell, but many of those who are in prime roles now or soon will be have served in multiple changeovers of ruling bodies. They have learned what is necessary and what isn't, and that's why they wanted to come back and achieve change without the chaos and bloodshed of your past. We know your patience is exhausted waiting for NESARA to come and with it, the resignations of the US president and his administration.

Stop waiting and live fully and let NESARA lie! If you must think of it, think of it as a blueprint or a set of short- and long-term goals and not as the whole enchilada—yes, I know your expression—coming all at once. Processes in motion will be slower but just as certain in the results that NESARA intends. The house of cards that is the US Congress is falling like dominoes in slow motion behind the scenes. There are holdouts, and we can't say that we didn't anticipate this, but the many who are responding to the light—and light is our ONLY weapon!—will be helping us to influence the ones still on teeter totters. **July 26, 2005** PS. Suzanne, please add to my message that when we undertake important missions, such as assisting you all in this transition out of darkness into light, we DO NOT MAKE MISTAKES! The series of bumblings given as "reasons" that NESARA never gets announced time after time are just plain nonsense! Anyone who knows the truth of us realizes that, but the people whose discernment is just developing could see us as part of the problem, because however could bumblers be part of the solution?

December 31, 2005 I bid you "Good evening," Suzy, with thanks for receiving me in these last hours of your

year 2005. I ask that you send out my message with the
next one from Matthew.

This is Hatonn speaking in my capacity as director of
communications between Earth and all points elsewhere
during the era of Earth changes. You may know of me as
commander of an intergalactic fleet. That is another of my
"hats," but in this moment, my focus is communications
about another area of my activity, what you commonly
refer to as NESARA. I am here to give a definitive
statement in particular, but not exclusively, to all who have
been working diligently to initiate NESARA's wide-reaching
reforms and now don't know what to believe.

The *National Economic Security and Reformation Act*—
please note this *accurate* name—is as real as anything else
on Earth, so to all skeptics, please put to rest the impression
that it is merely a wish in the minds of some who intensely
desire a legislated remedy to your world's problems.
Nevertheless, that view does have some validity. Like
everything else in the universe, this Act's formation was
preceded by and manifested through thought forms. You
are inured to living within manmade laws, so we had to
put this within an acceptable legal framework. In
accordance with universal laws, the framework had to
specify means to achieve the Act's objectives so the
universe knows what situations to present in aid of
manifesting the desired results of peace, justice, equitability
and accountability starting in the United States and
extending worldwide.

That said, a great deal of DISinformation about
NESARA has been promulgated by various sources to
discredit this Act. That isn't surprising, because its
provisions strip them of political and economic control
over you. But it's unfortunate that NESARA has become

better known through those means than the correct information from knowledgeable sources such as Matthew. Approximately two and a half years ago we asked him to issue our collective statement that described NESARA as the divinely inspired co-creation of highly evolved beings on and beyond Earth to engender good will among her humankind and a fair share of good fortune for all. Food for the spirit is not enough for the majority of your population, who are oppressed and deprived, and NESARA was born of Earth's desire for betterment in the lives of all her resident souls.

In that message Matthew also spoke of Dove's credible reports, and at that point and for a time afterwards, she did faithfully report what she was told by lighted souls both on and off-planet. That changed about two years ago, when it became evident from our higher vantage point that the control of the ones we call "dark" was sufficient to prevent NESARA's implementation well past the optimum universal timing. Ah yes, the movement of celestial bodies has great bearing on what happens in your world, and they don't wait for procrastinators. To adhere to that timeframe, we opened new avenues to accomplish the identical aims of NESARA, more slowly but with equally certain outcome.

Dove's preoccupation with the success of the program in its exact design that was the basis of her reports clouded her receptivity to the new multifaceted course. In spirit this course is aligned with NESARA's provisions, but it can move independently of the Act's restrictive legal require-ments that the dark ones were manipulating to their advantage. Dove's dedication that had been admirable in its fervor and exhaustiveness turned into egotism with her choice to report what she felt would be more effective than our new direction. Light and egotism aren't compatible, and with her change in attitude, her light faded. She lost her former high connections along with her ability to discern that she was reaching dark entities or to properly evaluate information from Earth sources. The natural consequence is the inaccurate information she has been issuing.

Until a very short time ago that made no difference at all in the "behind the scenes" progress. Although further efforts in the old direction were futile in one respect, in another, and far more important respect, they were powerful. The light generated by the *intent* of all involved enabled the "lift-off" and then sustained energy momentum of the new processes to fulfill NESARA's objectives. But Dove's recent contentions that are strikingly without factual basis have caused considerable confusion. Introducing this kind of energy attachment is not helping to propel our activities' momentum to surge pace, and that's why I am telling you what has transpired. The *energy of your belief* that NESARA's objectives ARE being met, albeit on a parallel track, is as imperative now as before.

This is not a place for anger or shame, but rather sadness that the soul who once correctly reported on NESARA unwittingly veered off the light course. We honor Dove's service within her original mission and we beam intense light for her return. We beam the same to the dark entities that falsely claim to be me or other beings of light, and to the receivers who believe them and send out that false information. Be keenly discerning about *all* channeled messages! Especially in this late phase of Earth's transition out of third density, knowing what is true and what is false is critical *for your own sakes!* We urge you to look beyond the mass of muddled information about NESARA, Second Coming, First Contact, disastrous destruction to land masses, nuclear war potential, a dying planet—*listen to what your souls are telling you!*

Hold within your hearts the vision of the world you want for yourselves and your families, for all the inheritors of Earth:

> *A world where peace and love replace war and hatred; where governments are led by just, prudent and spiritual women and men, not power-mongers led by darkness; where fair distribution of all resources replaces the extremes of egregious greed and desperate poverty; where universal and planetary truths replace the web of lies that has controlled your lives.*

The concept and intent of NESARA is to help you create that world on Earth. You do not have to know of this Act or, if you do, you don't have to believe in its actuality — *wanting the same intentions that it embodies is what counts.* IT ALREADY HAS COUNTED! You are reading this in the early days of your year 2006, when wars, suffering, tyranny, corruption and the like can be seen wherever you look. But *in this very same instant* in the continuum, where everything is NOW, Earth is peaceful and beautiful and all of that negativity is gone. She has reached her chosen destination where low-vibration manifestations don't exist. The world of your vision, the "future" world you are helping to create right now, *already IS!*

February 1, 2011

Suzy: Matthew, there's less than two years until 2012 ends and time is speeding up. The truth about our space family, our origins, religious dogmas, the Illuminati — the truth about everything that's going to be shocking to most people — still hasn't come out and there's not much evidence of major changes in governments or the global economy. Can we get everything done in time?

MATTHEW: Mother dear, you've heard MANY times
that Earth's entry into fourth density is absolutely *assured!*
However, expecting all the glories of her Golden Age to be
on the threshold of the year 2013 would be a false expectation
—your world will continue on a "new and improved"
track that will be an amazing adventure! That all forms of
negativity, all the dark activity and Illuminati control, will
be gone by then is a *realistic* expectation, *and it will be met!*

The tenacity of the dark minds still in power, which is
keeping those truths under wraps and profound changes
still simmering behind the scenes, is breaking. Only
tattered remnants of the once powerful and cohesive
Illuminati global network still are operating, but enough so
that there is not yet much evidence of the phenomenal
turnaround that you shall indeed see by the end of 2012.
What is evident in your world is that people are seeing the
power of their numbers and they are demanding change,
working for change; and in Earth's field of potential, the
momentum of this collective energy is unstoppable. This
doesn't mean an abrupt end to violence, corruption, tyranny
and deceit worldwide—that will come incrementally.

It will be a bumpy ride for many as shocking revelations
come forth and essential reforms quickly follow. With
everything in the universe being accelerated, heads will be
spinning as people try to adjust to one huge change after
another. Knowing that all of the tumultuous happenings
are propelling Earth into her Golden Age, lightworkers are
well prepared to weather the coming months and to help
those who are foundering. Keep foremost in your
thoughts: *The world you are creating right now already IS in
the continuum!*

PART II

VOICES OF EARTH

SOME VOICES CREATING OUR WORLD

The energy in every single one of our thoughts, feelings, words and actions attracts similar energy in the universal consciousness and pulls more of its kind back to us. Individually we are creating our own lives in every moment as collectively we are creating our world. And it doesn't end here. The energy we continuously are generating affects in kind the entire universe – no wonder our space brothers and sisters are eager to help us "light up" Earth!

The selected excerpts of correspondence I've received are representative of the ways people are reacting to our world today. If in these messages you find echoes of your heart – remembering that love is what heals – you know the powerful influence you are having on Earth and beyond.

The metaphor of the ocean, the cups and the drops gave me a wonder-full understanding of Soul. You and Matthew have brought a beautiful gift to the world and it will help in bringing about change to many. One heart at a time this world is changing.

This is Isabel writing from Switzerland to say that Matthew's messages especially touch me each time he presents to us something we simply did not imagine, did not know from our Earthly awareness, and I think we all unconsciously long for. Something so beautiful we can find it only in our hearts, if not experienced in our daily lives. For example, these civilisations who communicate with tones of the most magnificent beauty hardly imaginable on Earth ... it must constantly caress the soul and wake up love in the heart. Now this is WONDERFUL!

As Matthew reveals the power of deeply felt love, it gives us an idea of how sublime love's reality is and encourages us to manifest this ourselves. The inspiration of his messages motivates us to unfold our divinity by surrendering to love and acting from our hearts. I have read all the Matthew Books, and that is how I have felt since the first. Sometimes I have tears flowing, this is how greatly certain things he describes touch me and reveal to me what I long for. Sometimes I have a sweet smile and feel comforted to know that it already is a reality in a different dimension and is on its way in ours. And it makes me realise how much this is what we humans are meant to achieve here and now, how much this gives a sense to all we are going through.

This urge to manifest the divine is our motivation to jump over our own shadows to reach out in *love*. With this most heartfelt gesture of caring that radiates the beauty of the soul, we shall bring harmony to our world.

We, here in Antwerp, Belgium, did read some messages from Matthew. They are so pure, so full of Love, and we wonder if there are given more messages and where we can find them. Love you, His Belgian fans

As an Englishwoman who converted to Islam after moving to Malaysia and marrying, I've found that your books have helped me immensely in finding the perspective I needed to stop the wobbling between despair/anger and delight in life. I know what is going on! Finally!

For me the most important part has been a helpful perspective on Earth's incarnate life forms, their free will and their buffeting by the forces swirling around them. It is so helpful to understand that experiencing what I interpret as "negative" might be a necessary part of the balancing process. The central idea of achieving balance has been most helpful. Now when I feel whatever seemingly external situation is trying to push me over (like playing with one of those childhood toys that always bounces back), I can pause and ask myself where the imbalance comes from, where the balance lies. (That part about homosexuality being an experience to achieve balance was very enlightening.)

I sense that if I can collect everything within me, recognise everything as a part of the whole, be inclusive and never exclusive, then any hand would just pass through the "toy" and it wouldn't be swayed at all. I only sway in resistance to the hand that pushes! The stuff in your books about needing to synthesize both sides of any controversy in order to stop the negative energy perpetuating itself on both sides is in line with what I've learned about Love being inclusive.

Our study group met last evening and began the first book. We started with the glossary and some terms led into enhanced info for some of the group. The ones on dark energy and balance were timely for some of us, because we are working on compassion and the yin-yang concept. Our valley here is heavily peopled with dark-negative-evil energy which is very active and has been for the last several years. The definitive explanation of God and Creator is extremely helpful. We have a lot of walk-ins here, there has been quite a bit of UFO activity for several years, and it is a rigid Bible-belt area....interesting combination!

Thank you for the wonderful books. I have the privilege to red them and I think you are a shining person (of Light, Love and Faith). And that you have a lot of courrage. I am greatful to Matthew and all the E.T. who wrote these books (with you). These books confirm us a lot of things about God, Eden, Earth-Terra-Shan, the future and about....us. All these words are from a mother's hart. Thank you Suzanne for the great love and faith who leads you to God and...these books. God bless You and I send You all my love and respect.   Irina — a Romanian mother

The books are a joy and an inspiration, and challenging too. Matthew's and the others' messages are showing me more clearly what is light and what is darkness in my own life. I'm encouraged that smiles and caring and simple communications like these are light for this world. Also I see that certain energies in me are the darkness and need to be seen as such (gulp!). Hard to accept, but truly helpful if I'm to fulfill my part in this great change.

Please send me one more copy of Matthew, Tell Me about Heaven. My own mother is facing her transition now, and I just hope that somehow she can receive this energy and information that you're giving. Thank you.

I am a doctor in Italy who lost my 6 year-old child by a rare cancer 7 years ago and he helped me and my wife to overcome the grief by teaching us how to help others. I'm very impressed by your story on your site but I have a question in my mind: what validates your contact with Matthew? In other words, how can you give proofs that this contact is for real?

I'm totally astonished by reading your book and Jean Hudon's e-mail about how he was convinced of your contact with Matthew. I'm also amazed by the similarities among Matthew's information and my findings about the Afterlife. I too had in my mind your same question about the "research" of my son after his transition and I also didn't touch his body in the casket because I knew that he was not that icy corpse. There are a lot of feelings of yours that match with mine and I totally agree with you when you say: "grief is an intensely painful private journey." I used to say that even the grief due to someone's dog's transition is so deserving of respect, we can't measure it!

We too had a lot of messages through mediums and proofs about our son's happy life. There his job is to keep in touch with myself for other grieving parents. He told a medium that I am a kind of link between the Earth and the Skies and that he's always "behind my computer screen" to establish the contacts. I wonder if I found your site because of him.

Suzy, this is so right on, the warmth and humor the Masters and God *do* indeed have!

The description of your work with Matthew is helpful as I am trying to do some work with my past lives through a channel here in Israel. I am trying to solve a long-term, apparently ages-old soul-level problem. I understand that I lived in Atlantis with a group of people who were together responsible for the sinking of Atlantis over a period of time. We did not understand consciously that we were needed to do that because of the destructive way of life which had developed there. So apparently when I realized what tremendous destruction I and we had caused, I smashed a crystal (which was part of the mechanism I had been using??) and built a tremendous energy barrier around myself, apparently around my soul, if such a thing was possible—so that never in any future life would I be able to cause such destruction again.

I am now 72 years old, have meditated daily for the past 21 years and it is the basis of my life. It provides me with a beautiful grounding, love, and some kind of non-verbal guidance. But since my husband passed over last year, I have begun to understand that my main purpose in living now, alone, is to learn how to remove that barrier, and to continue to develop to the point where I can really help the other souls who participated in the Atlantis destruction, and those who were hurt by it. This has been a new experience, especially since I am a very active person, doing projects about peace and Arab-Jewish relations.

I am almost through the third 'Matthew' book and what a wonderful ride it has been! Off hand, I cannot think of any three books that I have read, and it has been many, that have the powerful impact that you and your son Matthew are giving the world. I am most grateful.

And that message that Matthew gave on the progress of the NESARA legislation. My wife Maureen and I devoted our 30 years together working in the courts and forming a common law venue towards these goals that the law entails. We were with the Farmers when they received their win in 1993. Unfortunately, the very farmers that by agreement were bringing the 'Claims' movement to the public were rail-roaded with trumped up charges. Maureen and I helped to support them in court. This then gave birth to NESARA, as it could not be done by any other means.

And sadly, I lost Maureen to cancer almost 2 years ago. She was a massage therapist and healer herself. Boy, do I still miss her. I'm sure you can understand. Thank you again for these very needed books.

hello, my name is Ann. i was thrilled to receive information about matthew's books and the information right from his light source about sept 11th. like so many i have been very troubled by all this pain and hatred, I can feel it right to the core of my spirit. the past two weeks it has invaded me from within and i have struggled with a fatigue that has dominated my whole being...the pain, the hatred that reaches out to me from every direction is overwhelming. matthew's words are a beam of light and hope and a greater understand. each time i read them i learn more. i would like to wish you and matthew peace and love, it is God's work you do, opening the gateway between life and death and more, bringing peace and hope to so many.

The information is so wonderful and so important. Sometimes it can be so hard to keep your heart in the right place. I try and try and try and try to get the message across, but it has been extremely difficult. I live in the northern foothills of the Blue Ridge Mountains, in the deepest heart of the Bible belt. You would think folks here would have better thoughts, but they are closed-minded, and — well, it gets very hard to reach them. I have pointed out your web site and the Matthew books to everyone I can. Most brush me off as some kind of nut case. The minister at the church I attend doesn't want to listen to the information or believe it. When I talk with my good friend who is studying to become a minister, I can feel her heart closing off the real message being brought forth. Sometimes it can feel so hopeless, I just want to sit down and weep.

However, I keep plugging because the message is so very important. I work at a close custody prison and I have talked a lot with the inmates about your books. They are

thirsting for information like this and want to know more.
But all I hear from the other officers is more violence. They
want the US to go over and wipe whole countries off the
face of the earth! Horrible thoughts! So very, very sad.

Matthew is saying *what so many others are saying, that
the agenda is fear, mind control and world domination. The only
'weapon' we have is more light!! It is wonderful to see many
waking up to the Truth. Ascension has begun and is assured.
Thank God. These ARE exciting times to be alive! I feel strongly
that it is very important for us to be able to hold our light presence
NO MATTER WHAT. I thank you and Matthew for presenting this
information and spreading the Truth and the Light.*

I am Monika, living in Austria next to Vienna and I am
very happy about your books. Many people in my country wanted
me to tell them about the cover with Matthew's picture and I partly
had to translate various passages while we have been discussing
the different questions of you and Matthew answering them. This
helpful information, it really gives us a much wider picture of what
life on this earth is all about. It also gives much comfort to people
who lost a loved one recently. In behalf of quite some people in
Austria I thank you very much and wish you many more beautiful
hours with Matthew, your beloved son.

I have just finished reading this excellent material
from Matthew. I was so excited to read the quality of it. I
find it to be filled with valuable information that cannot be
found in many of the channeled works out there. This is
precisely what I have been trying to tell others in my feeble
way. I have about 4-6 months left to live. I have my own
small group of souls I pass on material to, and it is my most
fervent desire after my transition, to be able to bring forth
valuable correct information to one of my family members

or someone in the group that can receive my messages.

If the church officials would only preach the REAL truth and quit this stupid game of keeping man separated from his Divinity, which by the way, makes us all bastards of the universe to hear them speak. It would help a great deal to allow man to accept the concept of reincarnation and release the fear of this horrid father and one life and one death, man might actually straighten out and get a hang of what life is all about. Unfortunately, Matthew is correct, it is all about power and control, right down to the stock markets and the wars small and large. FEAR is control.

My friend is very impressed with the heaven book and will be forwarding it to his friend. My mother has loaned her book to many friends who have lost a loved one. They find it very comforting. I gave a copy to my sister who lost a husband last year and she too found it comforting.

This is Birgitta in Sweden and I want to thank you for the uplifting and soothing messages from Matthew that you forward to Jean [Hudon]. When I see in the summery of Jean's weekly dispatchings that there is a message from Matthew I jump to it straightaway. Deeply in my heart I thank every lightworker that contributes to the uplifting process we are in and who gives clarity to this rather uprooting and unsettling period of time. May peace always abide in our hearts and may we always feel surrounded with the Light manifested by the infinite number of divine beings that exist everywhere.

I love to hear what Matthew has to say and am glad that his messages are being heard. I'm glad to know that whether there is an actual legislative act or not, that the "spirit" of NESARA is in the energy fields! I will add to the belief field that we CAN have that kind of world and soon. My partner and I are working on that on a smaller level by educating people about how money REALLY works and helping people eliminate credit card debt and taxes, and then begin to build their assets NOW, without waiting for anything. Being free of the energy drag of debt and taxes frees people's spiritual energy amazingly! They begin to fly after that and claim their personal power and sovereignty.

Thank you for your beautiful book and sharing your conversations with your son Matthew. Your book deeply touched me. My son, Mike, passed away on January 4th. Because of the severity of his injuries in a car accident, he remained in a coma. During his short time in hospital, we noticed some signs of contact; his hand moved softly under mine and his eyes moved. On the morning of January 4th, I told him that a million people were around him thinking and praying for him. I told him that it was alright and that he should take his wings and fly. I thanked him for every-thing we had shared. He then opened his big brown eyes, looked straight ahead, and then closed them. I said to his nurse, 'He is going to sleep now'. I knew that he was not alone; nor was I.

Since that moment, I have been living absolutely knowing that Mike is around protecting me and all of his friends. In March, a woman with a sixth sense had contact with Mike. His awareness of my life is unbelievable. He is still very concerned (he always was) and advises me. We both miss each other enormously, especially not being able to touch. Reading your book has given me so much help and hope for the future.

Further, it reconfirms that 'There Is Far Far More' than we all realize. I have always told everybody that my example is proof that this statement is true. Knowing and realizing this does not change the fact that I MISS HIM, but I still live, walk my two dogs, eat, cry gallons of tears, sleep, and even laugh. I know that I cannot touch him for the rest of my life, but knowing he is there gives me so much comfort. Thank you for sharing your experience and books with me. Your books MUST be translated in Dutch so people here in the Netherlands can read them. If I could be of any assistance, please let me know.

I'm most grateful for Matthews' message of June 30th. I thought it was such a beautiful gift to our country, to come along during the July 4th celebrations. It certainly changed the way I looked at the 4th, and what to wish for our country's birthday! What a special present!

Since I've been immersed in your 3 books, I feel the distance of almost 20 years since my near-death experience shrinking in time, to almost feel like I don't know where I am. I'm recalling brief bits of experiences that over the struggles of 20 years were all part of my existence. Now, because of what I've read, I can look at things in a different perspective. Many of the "guests" who have spoken in your books were more in keeping with what my experiences were like. I never found any identity with all the near-death conferences, speakers and the few books I've come across, until yours. Sort of like a validation to my aching soul. I can never thank you enough!

I found out about you and Matthew through Jean Hudon's site. I ordered the book from the States (Tell me about heaven) — I live in Germany — and I want to thank you and Matthew a thousand times! In this life I am a doctor, doing homeopathy, but now am terminally sick myself. This information is such incredible solace and joy to me, and it was also so much fun reading it. There is a part of me that is really curious what I will be assigned as a job when I get there.

I was reading page 172 of Matthew book #3---where God is speaking to you and says 'ciao' – adding, HisHer preference was saying 'toodle-oo' but knew you would think you were just imagining it. I was sitting in a restaurant nearby the quaint village of Saxen, here in Austria, reading this. As I paused to digest and SAVOR what God was saying, I focused on the word 'ciao.' As I did, at that precise moment, a regular customer in that restaurant, opened the door to leave, near the coffee table where I sat, but paused and smiled at me...and said a loud, clear, 'ciao!' – and I almost fell out of my seat (SMILE). Since reading this book, I have gotten friendlier with God – yesterday during one of my walks, I asked if God would send me signs that I would NOTICE that He/She was 'around.' It felt like God said 'ciao' directly to ME at that moment – which of course He/She did...through that customer. What a nice JOLT!!

I have been waiting my entire life to have access to the information that I have begun reading in *Revelations For A New Era*. I cannot believe I have finally found this book. I have always prayed that the Truth would be placed in front of me one day, and for the last 10 years, I have been searching and searching. I feel that now the puzzle is near completion, or at least the first chapter of the puzzle. Last night, when I received the book and read the intro papers that came attached [*Matthew's WESAK message*], I was filled with a tremendous wave of relief; a feeling that finally a huge project in my life was accomplished: what I had been searching for, for so long, was finally found. I live in Canada and am twenty-one years old, which may seem young, but it feels as if I have been searching for so much longer.

Some of the things spoken about in those intro sheets struck me so deeply, confirming things that I have felt I need to do and accomplish in this life. Anyhow, it's too complex to explain for now.... However, I wrote to thank you, sincerely and deeply, and especially to Matthew, and whoever listened to my prayers and helped in bringing this information into my life. It answers even some detailed questions that are very if not exactly, similar to my own. For instance, the questions on autistic people and the mentally handicapped, as well as those becoming brain-damaged at birth. Please, in your next conversation with Matthew, relay my thoughts (in brief), and thank him.

Thank you, Suzy and Matthew. I have enjoyed your messages for the past year or so. I am a practicing Chiropractor and alternative health provider in Missouri. I am amazed everyday at the messages I get as I work to interface patients with their own healing abilities. I figure I am getting about 80% and often wonder why the other 20% won't come through. I guess Matthew answered that for me today, that if people's soul contracts don't include being healed, we can't help them.

This message from Matthew is very very worthy...it rings totally true for me. This message is one of the best that has come thru. It is how we "negotiate" out there in the Universe in the council meetings. I am one who stands up a lot for Truth and says things like "This cannot go on" or things like that. I understand opposing and holding the balance. I have never heard it put so succinctly before. It is something not well understood by lightworkers. It is so true, lightworkers are generally all strict and finger-wagging about what is right, or they are the opposite and do not want to get involved at all in "negativity." So I thank you for this!!!!!!!!!!!!

It's difficult for me to express all that I feel and have gained from these books...they have given me so much. I perceive so many things differently and approach life so differently. When many things occur that I would have before viewed as roadblocks or impediments, I now see as opportunities. Do I always succeed in the correct and loving response??? NO! But I do take a second thought and look and try to correct the original response. Do I always succeed then? NO - - but the difference is that I am working on all of that and at least I now have the information and map as to the proper road to travel in order to get to where I want to be. All of the information from Matthew and the other lovely "energies" are always with me - - every day, every moment.

Oh - - Suzy, try not to ever be concerned about whether or not the information that Matthew is imparting to you is true and correct - - it "rings" like a beautiful bell in the soul when I'm reading it - - it's very easily recognizable! I know that you feel a great responsibility to those to whom you are imparting it, but you need not worry - - - it just settles so quietly and gently in our individual corner of light! - - like a homing pigeon!

It's been an amazing experience to find that some of my "views" and "feelings" about certain things turn out to be right on cue - - like God being as He is - - I JUST KNEW HE WAS MORE "APPROACH-ABLE" than we had been taught - - - and somehow, I knew he had a wonderful sense of humor and I wasn't shocked at His use of "hip" language at points. I SMILE when I think of it - - - - a giggle actually, filled with LOVE/LIGHT. I can't even begin to express or share all that I feel because of Matthew's and your books!

Thanks to your and Matthew's purchase of the "poor, struggling, little potted plant," I repotted some of the same in our office and shall see to it that they receive tender, loving, nurturing care! You see, that is just an example of how differently I see things now - - - that "under the magnifying glass, clarified view" of how "the connection" literally touches EVERY TINY LIVING THING! And maybe the greatest gift of all is that I share all of this with someone every day! [South Africa]

I have just come back from a trip for my grandson's Bar Mitzvah and reread the material in the books. What Matthew says makes sense, about not letting the dark thoughts take over our minds and psyches. I do have a tendency to let my anger boil over when I hear false things being said, especially in politics. So it will be hard for me 'to keep my equilibrium' when I hear obvious untruths. But I will try, and already I have made myself a promise to read only uplifting material before going to bed, and that is a help, but it will take some work to do it! And sending love and light to dispel the dark influences will also take some doing, but I am going to make the effort.

I feel so completely at home with the spark of God that is within me, and each and every one of us. I have always felt that I didn't need an intermediary to speak with God. God, he/she, dwells within each and every one of us, and we are all interconnected. Which is why when I see or hear of anyone, anywhere, hungry, mistreated, hurting in any way, I feel it as though it were me.

Now, my problem is how to deal with the disgust and, yes, even hatred, for those dark forces which bring such pain and suffering to the world, and promulgate fear, which, in turn, allows the dark forces to reach their goals of dominating the planet. But you and Matthew give me such hope that other planetary forces are watching over us, and are here to help us. It makes my heavy heart so much lighter!

Thank you so much for making my life so happy. I have always believed in God and heaven but now I know it is true. Never stop writing books together with your son. I love every word that is spoken. I will never ever forget this experience. May God bless you and Matthew for enlightening this planet forever.

My son was killed at the age of 19 almost 6 years ago. He was a beautiful, beautiful person, and the loss to me was indescribably difficult... but you know that. I would give so much to have the kind of communication with Christopher that you have with Matthew.

I have often felt that my work here (psychiatrist) is somewhat of a preparation for working on the other side to help people through. For a long time I have felt that. I wouldn't be a bit surprised if that is what Christopher is doing there.. Well maybe, anyway. He was such a caring, insightful person when he was here.

I honor your beautiful son and you, and your magnificent mission.

I HAVE JUST READ MATTHEW'S WESAK MESSAGE WHICH I APPRECIATE AND HONOUR. I CAN DEFINITELY RELATE TO THE MESSAGE AND I AM SO GRATEFUL FOR WHAT I CAN ALSO SAY IS A 'VALIDATION' FOR US HERE IN THE PHILLIPINES. KINDLY PASS THIS COMMENT ON TO HIM. AND TO YOU, THANK YOU SO MUCH FOR OBLIGING MY REQUEST AND FOR DOING WHAT YOU AND MATTHEW ARE DOING FOR EARTH AT THIS TIME.

Matthew's message is very important information, and I completely agree... discernment is imperative. I have always had problems with channels who say we should never look at tv or read the news. I feel it's imperative as global/cosmic citizens that we pay attention to what's playing out in the world, but with a level of discernment that looks beyond the surface of what we're being told to what's really going on.

I really don't think that is so difficult. It doesn't take much of a leap to see that we're watching the breaking down of old energies so the new can come in. I think as world citizens committed to planetary evolution, to really be about our work, we need to "know what we're looking at" (to quote my spiritual teacher), to have great integrity of interpretation, and to assimilate as much of the big picture as our human brains can allow.

It is so very complex, no one "channel" has the entire picture. It's more like a beautiful puzzle with many pieces floating around...and it's up to us to assimilate as much of this information as we can with integrity, wisdom, and through the nuances of our hearts tuned to compassion, love, and integrated Soul wisdom.

I have just visited your website, Suzy, and devoured what's there. It moved me to tears and I want to tell you I am so grateful to you and to Matthew. I will be talking about it in the Intuitive Mastery class I will be giving tomorrow at co-housing project just outside of Vancouver BC. Such an interesting time to be alive.....God bless.

I received lots of validation in your book for thoughts and teachings we have received, which is always comforting, as I'm certain you understand. As for the beings from another dimension/ star/planet who may inhabit a physical body, I actually know and teach so many of them that we have lost count!! We call them Starborns and there is a great section on them in *The Power of Love.* Our perspective is not "do they exist?" but rather, "what are the issues they have to deal with because they are not from here and have to live in a body ["meat suit" as some of them refer to it!!] and on this 3d plane. It really is hard for them, and we do what we can to make things a bit easier so they can get on with their Mission.

Illuminations for a New Era lets me feel very close to you although from my home in Australia, you are half a world away. I can understand your queries and concerns, and by this book you are a focus for many who are asking the same questions. The answers have come at a time when the need has never been greater. We are on the brink of a great awakening, an awakening that is imperative for the people of Earth if we are to lift our vibrations along with the planet.

PART III

SYNCHRONICITY

THE IMPORTANCE OF SYNCHRONICITY

Matthew

Your dictionary definition of synchronicity is sadly lacking. Synchronicity is nothing less than the universe in operation! What you perceive as random events, chance meetings, good or bad luck, isolated incidents, and especially what you call "coincidences" actually are energy in motion in perfectly defined and aligned directions to achieve specific results.

The synchronous process is like a stretch of dominoes on end—when the first falls against the second, a chain reaction flows until the last domino has fallen. While that is the simplest way to explain the workings of synchronicity insofar as one situation affecting the next and the next and so on, it is not an accurate explanation because the domino line had a first and last object. Synchronicity has no beginning and no ending—like the universe, it always is in motion—and synchronous happenings are not as obvious as a straight line. True, certain happenings in a lifetime stand out from the myriad others because of their greater importance, and direct tie-ins to those may be held in significance as well, but those, too, are surrounded by the "before" and the "after."

Synchronicity is the series of situations required to manifest the intended result of all the players. Please don't take offense at my term "players." If you could know the profound importance to your soul of your consciousness acting upon your variety of inspirations, motivations and intuitions, yet the simple reason for ALL the happenings, you would understand that Earth is a stage for all of you to play out the karmic roles you chose. The "importance" is the soul's chosen mission that is being relayed to your consciousness via those nudgings; the "simple reason" for all happenings is that you manifested them by your free will choices.

There is no limit to the number of players, no limit to the events in the proper sequence, and no limit to the distance that may separate the people involved. Usually the players have no awareness of their indispensable link in the chain reaction, and most often it is only in retrospect that individuals may realize that a series of seemingly unrelated people and events had led them to exactly where they are. But other times, at least in a small pocket of a lifetime, the players do recognize how others' meaningful entry into their lives had a profound effect.

You do of course participate in synchronous happenings, but you are not responsible for creating the circumstances or contacting the people who will be the links. Countless sources of energy come into play for each life, arranging the opportunities for connecting the links. But as always, free will is honored, so at each "open door" — or, new acquaintance or event — everyone may respond as he or she wishes.

My mother has been given guidance by the Council of Nirvana, acting on the selection by God of all material in the Matthew Books, to include in this one the stories of some who have written about the effects of the books and my posted messages in their lives. It is unlikely that all see the synchronicity involved, and it is not a requirement that they do. However, the value of recognizing that nothing happens by coincidence cannot be emphasized too strongly. It invites — *compels!* — you to look at your life in a new light by understanding the significance of the synchronous threads that have woven its design.

When you realize that happenings are purposeful, that they are guidelines and open doorways to karmic completion, you can proceed with more confidence, more excitement, more fulfillment and joy as you live this life in preparation for the next.

STORY OF THE MATTHEW BOOKS

Suzanne Ward

As an example of how synchronous events may happen, I was asked to tell you the story of the Matthew Books. Of course the synchronicity didn't start with the Internet, but without that I can't imagine how this story and the readers' stories selected for this book could have been told. Even more so, how the books themselves could have become known.

As Matthew mentioned, there is a "before" and an "after." In this case, the "before" is my soul level mission and life's journey that led to these books and Matthew's messages on the Internet, and the readers' journeys that led them to find those. The "after" continues for all of us—the ways this information affects our lives.

But I have to begin at a more current point than my pre-birth agreement or even my "backdoor" entry into journalism at age 39, and I think the best place is my connecting with Jean Hudon. A friend forwarded one of his EarthRainbowNetwork compilations, and after reading what a contributor wrote about cetaceans' highly evolved souls and their vital role on the planet, I felt a "nudge" to e-mail that writer Matthew's message that said the same. As a courtesy, I copied Jean. After a few brief e-mail exchanges, he asked if Matthew would suggest comforting words he could give his neighbors whose young daughter had recently taken her life.

Matthew did and, to my dismay, he offered more: If the parents were receptive to telepathic communication and would send the girl's name, he would contact her and give me a message to pass on to her parents. Making soul contacts is not Matthew's and my mission. To me his seems boundless, but mine is simply receiving information and organizing it for publication, *not* the heavy emotional responsibility of receiving a message from someone in Nirvana and praying that it will make sense and give solace to the family.

Jean's neighbors were eager to hear from their daughter, and Matthew told me she wanted to speak with me herself. A lovely young girl appeared in my "mind's eye," spoke about her life and gave me a detailed message for her family. I sent that to Jean along with the girl's appearance. Her parents were elated—they recognized their child by her message and my description.

Next Matthew told Jean that specific chapters in *Matthew, Tell Me about Heaven*, which along with *Revelations for a New Era* was being produced by an on-line publishing service, could also be helpful to his neighbors. Knowing their joy at hearing from their daughter, Jean was interested in both books and I sent him the text files. When the books were ready several months later, August 2001, he sent a sterling review to his large distribution list. That was the introduction of the books and their Web site, where they were free for downloading during the two months that followed.

Russ Michael's introduction to the books came about that same time, but by a series of synchronous events that began in Panama in April 1980. To explain those, I have to jump back to 2001, when new acquaintances who saw the books hot off the on-line press suggested that I contact

their friend in Texas, who had just opened an on-line book-
store. He replied that he needed the OK from his partner in
Austria, Russ Michael—it was to Russ that I had sent
Matthew's information about cetaceans and copied Jean.

Now back to 1980. Right after Matthew's memorial
service, when throngs of strangers were extending
condolences, a beautiful young girl clung to me, sobbing so
hard she couldn't speak. Despite my shock and grief, her
image was clear whereas all others were only blurs. I felt
that I wanted to comfort her and I wanted to know about
her and Matthew, but she was pushed away by the crowd.
My family didn't know who she was—Matthew had many
friends who were pretty blond girls. I thought about that
special one often in the weeks and months that followed,
but as the years passed, she faded from thought.

Nineteen years later I was at the Miami airport with my
daughter Betsy, who had been released from the hospital
after extensive surgery and was ready to return to her
home in Panama. When a lovely blond lady rushed up to
us, I had a flash of déjà vu, but there was time only for
Betsy to introduce Yoli and tell me that her mother also
was a channel and lived not far from my home in
Washington. Yoli hurriedly wrote her mother's telephone
number, I kissed my daughter goodbye, and they boarded
the plane.

Betsy's operation had been badly botched, and a week
later she had emergency brain surgery. I was asked not to
go to Panama because there was nothing I could do to help,
but I did think of something. The morning Betsy had left
the Miami hospital, I had gone to the gift shop to buy some
items she wanted and as I was walking out, I spied a book,
Celestial Healings. Impulsively I bought it, but since my
return home it had sat unopened on my bedside table.

Numbed by the news about my daughter, I leafed through the book and noticed that one of the energy healers had listed her phone number. I called Nancy Legett, who said she would start remote healing right away.

Even with that and Matthew's assurance that his sister would live, I felt desperate, and maybe in the spirit of one mother to another, I called Yoli's mother, Taylore Vance. She wasn't after all a channel like I, she was a healer like Nancy, and she also started directing energy to Betsy.

A week later Betsy had another emergency operation, and a week after that, she was flown to Boston for still more surgery. I was with her during those three weeks and saw the beginning of a long slow recovery. Matthew told me that Nancy's and Taylore's energy had helped him and others to preserve my daughter's life force.

The summer of that year the scene shifted to Vienna, Austria, where my son Eric was vacationing. Stopping at a red light, he glanced at the corner and saw Yoli, whom he hadn't seen for twenty years, not since his move to Chile and later, to Peru. During their afternoon visit, she told him that she had been with Matthew the day of his fatal crash. He had graduated a semester sooner than the other students, and that morning she was at home with a sprained ankle. After failing to convince her that she still could go bowling, he drove to his father's spice farm. On the way home, the Jeep ran off the road and wrecked in a rocky field.

I shared with Taylore what Eric had told me along with my memory of the sobbing young girl at Matthew's service. A few days later she called to tell me that girl was Yoli. Betsy never had talked with her about the crash, and with sensitivity to that trauma for our family, Yoli never had mentioned her last time with Matthew.

It was when Bob and I met Taylore and her husband that I gave her the books and she told me to contact her friend in Texas, whose partner then was Russ Michael.

Because the books' story really isn't unusual in the context of synchronicity, it's a good example of how seemingly unrelated connections flow through the years. It's the same principle—actually, the universal law—at work in every life. The next stories, which are not as ordinary, at least in my experience, offer more insight into the unseen forces at work in our world and how they affect lives well beyond our own.

Contributors whose surnames and contact information are given asked me to do that; it was my preference to use first names only for the others who also gave permission for their stories to be included.

A YOUNG MAN'S BURDEN

My communication with Richard started after Jean Hudon forwarded the following letter along with his personal note requesting Matthew's comments. Although I have been deeply touched by many writers' poignant stories, you'll see why the love and wisdom in Richard's had a singularly profound impact.

Richard's letter to Jean: My spirit guides told me during an out-of-body experience today about the importance of not holding onto bitterness and resentment—whether it's when other people treat you unfairly and do things that piss you off, or at the government or another country's government for the things they do, or even at life itself that seems more difficult than lives you see around you. Bitterness and resentment are heavy emotions to carry around, and when you die, there they still are within you because you never released them, only they are magnified and pull you down into one of the darker regions in the afterlife.

Your existence in the afterlife reflects not only the kind of life you lived in terms of physical actions, but also the kind of life you lived emotionally—how light-hearted you were, or how heavy of heart you were. Eventually, if you persist enough and do a lot of work on yourself, you may learn to leave the darker region for one that's a little lighter, but it is *much easier* to change how you are in the physical world. Why?

Partly because during your lifetime you're around a variety of people, but in the afterlife you gravitate towards the particular area where you're surrounded by people that were most like you during your life. A murderous person is surrounded by other murderous people; a betrayer is surrounded by other betrayers; a resentful, bitter person is surrounded by other resentful, bitter people; a person who's always gloomy is surrounded by other people who are always gloomy; a kind, forgiving person is surrounded by other kind, forgiving people, etc. The process is very exact, like magnetism. And because it's all you see around you, you don't have the good examples of more loving people there for you to observe and apply to yourself as you do in the physical world.

And part of it is because of how emotionally oriented the spirit world is. Because you're no longer wearing a physical body that tones down the emotions you experience, instead you experience emotions in their raw, much more powerful form. And this tends to make it more difficult to break emotional habits that you formed during your lifetime.

Another thing that can make it more difficult to progress to a lighter area in the spirit world is that by doing so, you will begin encountering people who are more loving, and this can be difficult due to shame and anger at self. Shame for your past unloving actions and anger at self for not having been a more loving person than you were, tend to make you rather comfortable in the area where you end up, so you have no motivation to make spiritual progress.

That's what I heard from my spirit guides, and it's why it's wiser to endeavor to change how you are now while it's easier, because you reap in the afterlife what you have sown during your life here *in all areas* — physical, emotional and mental. I realize that just because the principle of this is simple doesn't necessarily mean that applying it to your life is easy, but this is something that is infinitely worth striving for. And remember—it's never too late to begin, but it is better to begin sooner than later.

Matthew's response to Jean: Jean, my friend, greetings to you. I am pleased to have this opportunity to comment on the information Richard received from his spirit guides.

Indeed this is clear and correct. Actually, many of the passages in the books show that the energy registration of thoughts and feelings and free will actions in physical experiencing are exactly the pathway to the layer of Nirvana to which a soul automatically is led after transition. There is no escaping this! This is not judgment or punishment from any source, it is the "like attracts like" universal law in action.

The negativity of emotions such as bitterness, resentment, greed, envy, hatred and the like cannot enter the same layer of Nirvana as the light-filled emotions such as love, generosity, compassion and forgiveness because the energy vibrations are incompatible. The energy of souls with negative attachments must be free of those attachments before the souls can progress to the lighter layers of the realm, and light constantly is beamed to them to assist in their remembering process of their beginnings in the pure love of Creator. That love vibration is what removes the lower energy frequencies that automatically placed the souls among others of that same low vibratory essence. But free will reigns in this, too, and these souls can accept or refuse the light—that is, they may choose to rise into the higher density layers or remain where they are.

Earth is the ideal school for emotional experiencing.

Karmic relationships from the original populations are played out there rather than in Nirvana because it is in the planet's density that the acts were committed that incur the need for additional learning of the same chosen experiencing or for a "role reversal." Some souls have hundreds or more lifetimes learning just one lesson, say forgiveness instead of burning vengefulness. Others need to learn the emotions of a "victim" because they already know those of a "predator." The souls' understanding of this is clear in Nirvana through the life review process, and their subsequent choice of lessons for the next incarnate lifetime leads to family pre-birth agreements to the benefit of all principal souls involved. Well, to the benefit of those who listen to their soul's urgings once they actually are experiencing in body.

Richard's first e-mail to me: Hello Suzy. I was the one who wrote that e-mail to Jean. Something Matthew said seems as if it pertains to my experience: *"Others need to learn the emotions of a 'victim' because they already know those of a 'predator.'"*

Recently I was told by my guides that I am going to be murdered later this year, and this is to allow me to experience the opposite side of that coin so that I may learn on a deep level why it isn't wise to do that sort of thing. The guides said that I myself murdered in a recent lifetime (perhaps about 8 lifetimes ago) and then deeply regretted it and felt haunted by it for the rest of that life. They have given me this foreknowledge so that I am prepared ahead of time and won't hold onto bitterness and resentment when I pass over to the vaster planes. This is what inspired that e-mail that Jean forwarded to you.

May I ask Matthew a question through you regarding this matter, Suzy? There is something having to do with it that has been distressing me, and I would very much appreciate Matthew's perspective regarding it.

Richard's reply to my e-mail: Thank you so incredibly much, Suzy. Yes, foreknowledge is a part of this. Words can't express how much I appreciate finally having someone in the physical world to talk with about this.

I have wondered if I am to eventually be murdered no matter what in this lifetime for "karmic" reasons, or if it will happen only under certain circumstances, or if I have been misinterpreting things. I have wondered if my grandparents who live with me are to be murdered along with me, as there have seemed to be possible indications of that. If so, I have especially wondered how I can handle this foreknowledge wisely and lovingly both before and during the event considering how much I love them. In order to handle such a situation wisely, am I to not try to defend them? Am I to not try to prevent such an event from occurring to begin with in order to allow the lessons to be learned?

I don't want to make assumptions in asking my questions, so perhaps it would be wisest to simply ask Matthew if he would address this issue as well as give me some general advice for the next 6 months of my life.

Matthew's message: Dear soul Richard, yes, I can offer you answers in the areas you are questioning and I do so lovingly. Yes, it is necessary for you to experience what your soul has requested so that karmic completion of several unfinished lessons can be achieved simultaneously. It is NOT necessary that your grandparents suffer physically. They will mourn your passing and miss your physical presence, but depending upon how you live the remainder of your life as their grandson, they can find great comfort in remembering your approach to life and moving onward with excitement. They, like others of your family, friends and most influential others in your lifetime agreed to provide you genetically and environmentally an ambiance that promoted a loving, courageous, protective, unselfish, soul-searching nature.

You are correct that the foreknowledge is part of the pre-birth agreement — it is the most essential part for you in personage and for your soul's contentment about its leaps forward in growth. I cannot, nor would I wish to tell you how to spend the remaining part of this Earth lifetime, nor do I wish to infringe upon your free will choices by recommendations. What I do wish to impart to you is this wisdom that befits ALL souls: MAKE joy in each day! Share this with those whom you love dearly and let your radiance shine so that all who touch your life in any way are uplifted.

Richard, please consider this: Many experience their last months in severe physical pain and debilitation, or confinement in prisons, or virtual slave conditions under tyranny, or in war zones. Many live with hopelessness, fear and despair. Some have knowledge somewhat similar to yours insofar as physical life span and others live almost paralyzed by fear because they don't. Some souls come in knowing that their short lives will be starvation, disease and neglect. None has your choices to live freely and fully in each moment. Please think of your life in this perspective.

Please do not think I am making a comparison to try to convince you of your good fortune! It is not likely that consciously you view it as this — however, at soul level, it absolutely is! The request by your soul to complete in this lifetime the concentrated karma of many lifetimes was granted the divine grace of allowing awareness of a sudden, pain-free exiting if you manifest this by your thoughts, feelings and actions prior to that moment. That is why the foreknowledge provision of the agreement is paramount. Definitely I do not mean to focus on that end and be oblivious to LIVING, but the opposite—focus on the joyful moments on Earth!

You will arrive in Nirvana in a twinkling and it is up to you—how you live your remaining Earth life—to determine whether you are overjoyed to be back "on time" or feel disappointed that you missed the opportunity to leave those who love you with the comfort that you lived life to the fullest, lacking nothing meaningful.

Conditions prevailing on Earth will not be lasting much longer. There will be the understanding that a person's life doesn't end with the passage to Nirvana, but rather starts a new chapter of experiencing. As the planet ascends into lighter density, telepathic connections between there and Nirvana will be opened again, and travel back and forth will become commonplace. There will be the understanding of the inseparability of all souls throughout the universe.

Beloved soul Richard, despite my not wishing to influence you, my entirety is urging you to look upon what is ahead of you with a sense of fulfillment. Please do not dwell on sadness or "time" of leaving, but on the well-accomplished mission that ends with a wondrous new beginning! With tenderness and love, this is Matthew.

Richard's response: What Matthew said is so very helpful and applicable, to the point of my being pleasantly surprised a little. Very self-empowering and insightful, and lovingly so. I had asked myself what Jesus might do in such circumstances as I was dealing with and nothing much had occurred to me other than praying and asking for guidance. So I have prayed, and prayed.

I do my best to avoid making assumptions, but if what Matthew said is true regarding my grandparents not being involved in this upcoming event, then I breathe a sigh of relief. Admittedly, there's a little rush of adrenaline too, but I choose to unconditionally enjoy. Everything keeps going right, as I have started realizing more and saying recently.

It's kind of humorous. I wanted to move beyond this life to the vaster planes of reality, by way of suicide if necessary, for the majority of the time between '92 to earlier this year due to many challenging experiences in different areas of my life in a relatively short period of time. Then in April I made a leap in my spiritual focus and dedication to doing lightwork, and in the process of feeling this additional sense of purpose, I've no longer felt that same pull to move into the great beyond. And then the Divine Flow decides that I'm ready to go. Ah well, I faced my own death years ago and am ready to go at any moment.

I feel very happy and honored to make this connection with you, Suzy. To tell you a little about myself, I've been around for 28 years in this life so far. I was born and raised Catholic, and left the church at the age of 15 when I no longer agreed with its general way of seeing things. I then explored Wicca briefly, then the Tao Te Ching, then Buddhism. Starting my senior year in '93 I began reading channeled books from spirit teachers that innately made sense to me—from Seth, the Michael entity, and Lyssa Royal's channelings, and I grew so much from it. Starting in '96 I have greatly expanded from also integrating into my life the teachings of Orin, Bartholomew, Emmanuel, and some of Ramtha's teachings too, among others (although I don't agree with everything that JZ Knight channeled, some parts of it were very beautiful and insightful).

In recent years I have collected inspirational and insightful quotations from a variety of sources, as well as insightful parables, that have helped me to live even more happily and lovingly. I'd be glad to share them with you if you like.

The following are excerpts of some of Richard's subsequent letters:

One thing that I think most people don't realize is how big an effect their smallest actions have on the world. Each person's daily actions contribute far more to the global climate than anyone realizes. Usually in the science fiction I've seen it depicts such influence as fairly negligible when it comes to "ordinary citizens." But if you think about each person you interact with today, and each of the people they then interact with, and each of the people they then interact with, on and on and on, eventually you reach everyone on our planet, including the world leaders and people who are making a more direct impact on the lives of many people.

Let's say in this universe we inhabit, you say "Hi" to someone and comment on how much you like the design on the new shirt he's wearing. That affects him to whatever extent, and he thinks about it some afterwards, and it distracts him in a pleasant way from what he had been thinking about. So as he goes about the rest of his day, he thinks about things differently and interacts differently than he would have if you had just said "Hi."

Well, the difference is actually much greater than most people realize. Even if it begins as a small difference, it becomes a greater and greater difference over time. Each course would in turn affect the people that the person encounters due to how differently he interacts with them. And this would cause those people to be affected differently and to go about things differently afterwards—to however small or large extent. They in turn would interact with people differently afterwards and on and on this would go down the line until you've reached everyone all over the world except for the occasional recluse—but even hermits, too, are affected one way or another because these interactions affect the universe.

Your decisions about your attitudes come into play because those affect your interactions. Let's say that when you were in the shower, some shampoo got in your eyes. In one "universe" you allow this to dampen your mood— you get pissed off and gloomy. When you see that friend, you say "Hi," but you're feeling too glum to sound cheerful or comment on his shirt. But in an "alternate universe," you choose not to let the shampoo in your eyes dampen your mood—instead you laugh it off and begin whistling a little tune. Later on when you see your friend, your "Hi!" is lively and you are in the mood to comment on his shirt.

That's just a very simplistic example, of course, but it shows how a small difference ends up becoming a huge difference down the line. And that's why each person actually makes such a big difference in the world with moment-to-moment choices of attitudes and actions.

I suppose this awareness could paralyze some people with fear that they will do the "wrong" thing in their interacting with others and that will end up having a huge adverse effect on the world. But all we can really do is be ourselves and do the things we feel pulled to do. I've integrated this knowledge in such a way that I do my best to help others help themselves—like when it comes to leading a wiser and more loving life—based on the things I've learned from experience as well as what I perceive as wisdom from others (thus, my sharing inspirational/ insightful quotations and parables and other such material), and part of my intent is to have an overall beneficial effect on humanity and our planet.

I've misinterpreted the messages given to me numerous times over the years in my remembered astral experiences, due to often having to interpret symbolism and trying to read between the lines. I often got my hopes up and then experienced the resultant letdown when things didn't work out the way I had thought they might. And though it can still be kind of frustrating, I've learned over time to emphasize to myself before acting on my current interpretation of their messages to me: "I am creating no hopes regarding this. I am creating no assumptions regarding this. I am creating no expectations regarding this." But I do my best to apply that to my everyday life anyway.

The truth is, if it's going to happen, given the choice, I would rather have it happen sooner than later. In preparing myself for it, I look forward to the things that I will get to experience after passing on. But I've found that the middle path when it comes to not anticipating it, yet being prepared for it, can be a fine line due to fluctuating emotions and thought patterns. I focus as well as I can on being in the moment and enjoying it fully, but occasionally grisly possible scenarios still occur to me. I do my best to snap out of them ASAP and return my focus to the present moment.

Plus, I've been experiencing various challenges with my physical body for a while now. And though I've discovered that unconditional enjoyment is the key, I've still found it frustrating at times, and enjoy the thought of no longer experiencing the day-to-day challenges.

All judgment of others is self-judgment. All forgiveness of others is self-forgiveness.

Excerpt from my letter: .... *I think of you sometimes as my child, aware of what you know — how could I handle that? I'm not being morbid, dear, just feeling totally helpless to add something good to your life at this point I've entered it.* ....

Richard: Suzy, I understand in my own way. I sometimes imagine myself in your position, and am not sure what I would say other than general advice about enjoying life as much as possible, and offering as much loving support as I could.

I haven't told anyone else about this, not even any of my other spiritually awake on-line friends. I think it would be too distressing for most people — not just the possibility of it, but their asking themselves things like, maybe it's just a farce I made up to try and disguise my committing suicide or some such, and if they should tell my family or call the police or whatever. Most people seem to have a mentality of *"Keep everyone in the physical world for as long as you can regardless of what the circumstances are."* I have written a letter, however, that would be discovered if such an event were to happen, with the intent of helping to clarify things and give people some peace of mind in retrospect.

Suzy, here's an idea I'd like to share with you. Make a heartfelt prayer request for each of your family and friends who have passed over and ask that a beautiful bouquet of flowers be given to each of them. Something like, *"God, will you please manifest a beautiful bouquet of flowers with*

John Smith right now and tell him they're from my heart to his? Thank you."

Can you imagine how much it would mean to those in spirit to receive a loving gift like this from someone they know who is still in the physical world?

You also could do this for those you know who haven't passed over yet: *"God, when Jane Smith passes into Heaven, will you please manifest a beautiful bouquet of flowers with her at just the right moment and tell her they're from my heart to hers? Thank you."*

Imagine how much gentler and smoother it might help to make the transition and entrance into the spirit realm for your loved ones, and what a nice gift it would be to receive.

From my reply: Richard, I think your prayer idea is beautiful! Matthew just said he would like to say something here.

Matthew: My dear Richard, this is indeed a beautiful prayer sentiment and most worthy of sharing! I believe that you have insight into what greets each person who arrives in Nirvana's higher layers! Few on Earth have any idea of the welcome each soul receives in these light parts of the multilayered realm you call Heaven—it is a vast garden setting of incredibly beautiful flowers with sublimely mingling fragrances and music so splendid that you can correctly call it angelic. A gentler version of this panorama greets those in greater need of healing and custom nurturing, those who arrive with traumatic circumstances as their last memories of physical life, like war zones or other kinds of terror and brutality.

Souls whose free will choices in Earth lifetimes were darkly-inclined do not arrive in such an environment.

Please understand that I'm not referring to people whose chosen lessons SEEM dark by others' judgment but who actually undertook those roles willingly so karmic balance could be achieved not only by themselves, but also by all who are affected by their deeds. The people I'm referring to as "darkly-inclined" are those who chose lessons at soul level prior to birth and willingly and consistently ignored the inner voice of conscience and intuition, the soul's messages to the consciousness. These people are drawn by the universal law of "like attracts like" to the identical energy frequency in Nirvana as their Earth lifetime thoughts, feelings and deeds continuously registered.

The farther they strayed from their souls' chosen experiencing, the baser the energy they incur during the Earth lifetime and the correspondingly base layer of Nirvana to which they automatically go, with each layer of deeper density being less attractive, less comfortable. This is not punishment, it is "cause and effect," or, the natural result of their choices and the consequences. Love-light is constantly beamed to those souls, who may choose to accept it and rise into the more glorious parts of Nirvana or they may choose to refuse the love-light and remain in their surroundings.

I have digressed from my point, Richard, which is thanking you for your divine expression of prayer on behalf of souls here and those who will be arriving imminently. We in discarnate lives are NOT separated from you except in your minds! Our love—the highest energy in the universe—CANNOT be separated by what you perceive as "losing us." We are not lost to you! What you call death and we call transition is a lightning-quick change from physical life to life in etheric bodies in Nirvana. It is the *continuance* of life and our love bonds!

We value your prayers for us with the same thankfulness we felt when we were physically in your presence.

Richard: Eventually, Suzy, after you've passed over to the vaster planes, you are going to see my life and what all I've experienced, and you are going to see the love that you and Matthew have shined into it, and you may very well cry tears of joy.

Richard did send me a collection of his favorite writings and poetry. I asked him if a family member or friend would let me know when he died. He said they wouldn't know about our correspondence and he would send me a line or two every few days – when those stopped, I would know that he had met and welcomed his destiny. After a few assurances that he was still here, his e-mails stopped. Matthew told me that death came the instant that Richard was hit by a stray bullet and after being lovingly greeted in Nirvana, he joyfully began his fulfilling life in spirit. As I was reading Richard's story prior to the book's publication, he told me that himself.

A STARTLING E-MAIL

To: Suzy <suzy@matthewbooks.com>
From: Audrey E Davis <audreycraftdavis2.1@juno.com>
Sent: Friday, June 13, 2003 2:44 PM
Subject: Since this concerns your son, I thought you might
be interested.

Dear Suzy,

*I'll copy below the second e-mail I sent to Ron. My first
one was seeking his help in contacting you or Matthew on
behalf of my friend – I didn't have your e-mail address until
he wrote back two days later. His computer hadn't been working
and he hadn't received either of my messages until then.*

Dear Ron,

I must tell you this extraordinary result of my e-mail to
you last evening about a contact with Matthew and his mother,
when I was earnestly seeking help for my friend Cindy and
her daughter Jennifer and son-in-law Greg. The story is,
Cindy feared they were close to collapsing from lack of
sleep. Greg's mother had passed on and he was grieving.
So his mother came in to him from the other side and he, of
course, was delighted—until his mother never stopped. She
continued day and night. Greg would repeat his mother's
messages and Jennifer would write them down.

The problem was, all the family who were on the other
side decided to make Greg's mother their medium to get
messages through to their family members who are still on

Earth. None of them remembers the details of linear time, and the messages continued for many days and nights. This was why Cindy called me in desperation.

After I e-mailed you, I also sought help from a minister friend to see if she had any possible solution. Her willingness to see what she could do necessitated my call last night to Cindy, to ask if it was all right for the minister to call Greg that late at night. Somehow Matthew had picked up on my words in my e-mail to you, because by the time I talked to Cindy, Matthew already had communicated with her son-in-law and for the first time in many days he was sound asleep. She didn't know who Matthew was or what he had said to Greg, but she was so relieved that he had come to their aid.

I do not know what the message from Matthew was, but it surely was right, as all Matthew's messages are. Isn't this fantastic that he would get the message from my e-mail to you? None of Cindy's family had ever heard of Matthew, so he had to have picked it up that way. I wonder if I should tell Matthew's mother of this miracle? Please send me her e-mail address.

Love & Light, Audrey

PS. I must explain that Matthew died as a young teenager and years later came back to talk with his mother. He continues to come through to her and has asked her to put his messages in books, which she has been doing for a few years now.

Suzy, the next morning after I had written that e-mail to Ron, Cindy called to tell me that Matthew had just introduced himself to Greg and said he had come to help.

He assured him that he would take care of the problem, which he did!

You may like to know that I am a doctor of psychology, metaphysics and divinity.

Love and Light, Audrey

To: Audrey E Davis <audreycraftdavis2.1@juno.com>
From: Suzy <suzy@matthewbooks.com>
Sent: Friday, June 13, 2003 8:12 PM
Subject: Re: Since this concerns your son, I thought you might be interested.

Dear Audrey...

As you might imagine, your letter was a shock! I'm going to ask Matthew right now how this happened!

Matthew, hello, dear! You've read this message with me?

Yes, Mother, and I'll happily explain. The situation was relayed to me as I was not in Nirvana. The mother was so excited about the contact as were other family—and I believe even friends from past lives—that they did not realize what was happening in their enthusiasm for communicating. It was easy for me to let the mother know and understand, and she will not repeat that. With the accelerated energy flow on Earth, many soul contacts are opening in telepathic communication.

But why you? Why didn't someone right there in Nirvana clear up this situation, especially the soul who contacted you?

The ones who knew felt they did not know how to intervene in a "free will" connection and they know that I have handled these situations before.

Matthew, you've never mentioned anything like this to me!

Mother, dear, there is a great deal I haven't mentioned to you! Not to keep you unaware, but because we've talked about so many other aspects of my service that are on-going. That kind of situation is occasional.

OK! I'm sure the family here is very grateful for your help!

And I am grateful for the opportunity to help them! I know you need to get on with other things and that's all that needs to be said about this for the family's understanding.

Well, there you are, Audrey. Isn't life interesting?!

Love and blessings, Suzy

THE VISIT

A few weeks after Erik left, he sent me this, the latest entry in his chronicle about his life.

As a believer in taking an active role in humankind's evolution, being as we are at the doorstep to the next great leap, I find it so refreshing when along comes one who opens that door that others may see what lies beyond, perhaps even pass through. The Matthew Books have had a multiple impact in my life, much of it due to the synchronicity of how they came into my hands by Matthew's mother herself.

I called my dear friend and mentor, Violette, an extraordinary healer, following an urge I had neglected for a few days. During our conversation, she mentioned that Suzy Ward lived only a few hours from my sister's home, where my girl friend Susan and I were visiting. Violette thought perhaps that once again on the road, we might be able to swing through Suzy's area. I was then aware only that the Matthew Books existed, having read but snippets through Violette's e-mail. Her guidance thought Suzy and I should meet, and we did. Within the week Susan and I were with Suzy and her husband Bob, we became close friends.

Suzy and I spoke much of the synchronicity of our meeting, the days leading up to it, the visit itself with even tiny moments made so significant at her and Bob's wonderful and warm woodland cottage, made even warmer by their five dear old dogs. And more since then, the events which came to pass after our parting. Being a young man living a pivotal time of life, both in my personal and professional pursuits, I found that Matthew entered my life in perfect timing.

While the Matthew Books serve to enlighten us about the worlds we do not see and they expand our awareness of possibilities, Susan and I also discovered they bring with them even a greater service—a service of healing. After we left, Susan (who, on the second evening of our stay almost drove off into the night to who knows where) mentioned that perhaps the reason she was with me was to rediscover her own sense of spirituality. Matthew, and his dear mother, helped her remember there is more to life than the toils of daily existence. Susan released a good deal of fear, and our relationship was given time to mend. Though not yet entirely free of fear, our experience with Matthew and Suzy opened doors for us both, and Susan is now more willing to step forth into a new and brighter life.

Every religion offers a view of the afterlife, much based on penance and judgment. The fresh perspective Matthew reveals in *Matthew, Tell Me about Heaven* inspires me. When we can realize that once we leave this mortal plane, we meet not punishment, but rather continued learning, perhaps we can let love take the place of fear. For once, here is a vision of the "next world," free of hellfire and damnation, consequences of small "sins." We keep on growing, Matthew says, we keep on serving after we "die." I like that.

Raised in a Christian home, many hours have I spent in pondering the recorded words of Christ. Heaven in our hearts, Heaven on Earth is to come. I have always believed

God sends messengers to the people who need them. Who needs a messenger more than this society embraced by the pursuit of the almighty dollar, racing through each day to attend to petty matters of what consequence?

The words of Aeschyles in *Illuminations for a New Era* solidified this possibility of Heaven on Earth, for his world had achieved it. At the point of self-destruction, his people heeded the wisdom of their God-sent messengers and came back from the brink by creating a world in harmony. When human life on Earth evolves to a point of harmony and mutual goodwill, would we not consider Heaven to be here? Other peoples in this great universe have passed these same tests and learned the same lessons with which we now struggle. That offers hope. It cannot be long, then, until we on Earth remember our greater purpose in living and so transform our world into a place like Heaven. Or should I say, a place like Nirvana?

Matthew speaks in the hope we will listen, in the prayer we will hear. He has taught me much in terms of clarity and understanding, and he has confirmed that the battle we fight is indeed "not of flesh and blood." Matthew is a motivator for lightworkers, for we are not alone here in our quest to pierce the darkness. We are so not alone!

∞ ∿∞∿ ∞

THE SAME MISSION

Russ Michael wrote an impressive review of Victor Hosler's Angels in My Life, *and he sent that to Victor along with the suggestion that he look at www.matthew-books.com and get in touch with me. Victor did, and a number of e-mails and phone calls followed during July 2003. These excerpts from some of his early e-mails are a few examples of the synchronicity that kept emerging throughout our communication.*

Hello Suzy...

I went to your Web site an hour or so ago and still cannot adequately express my feelings. It had quite an emotional impact. It was probably from the somewhat sameness of our experiences.

You see, my entire personal experience similar to yours only began in January 2000 when my late and lovely wife, Claricé, came through to me spiritually five times between the 5th and 17th of that month. When I was believing that I was hallucinating or delusional after her first two visits, my very best teenage friend, who had committed suicide in 1963, also came through to me and said that Claricé had showed him the way. He had been trying to reach me since the late 1970s when I began doing past-life regressions as research for my novel on reincarnation. He came several times, with messages for his daughters, who were toddlers when he passed.

Next was my first mother-in-law, who died of an accidental drug overdose in 1967, with a message for her daughter that cleared up some questionable and ambiguous stories/thoughts about her death. Then the husband of a long-time friend who passed in 1977 brought me a message for his wife, and after that, I heard from the friend who gave the eulogy at Claricé's memorial service. He had a massive coronary the April following her passing and gave me a humorous, but brief message for his wife as well as telling me he had been neglectful regarding his health and had scheduled an appointment with a cardiologist that would have been the week following his death. *"Just a bit too late!"* he said. Then in August, a year following Claricé's passing, I began receiving communications from my angel guides. First Archie, my dominant guide, who said he felt that I was *"now ready to listen and believe."* I came to feel that I was definitely delusional and about to lose it all in my grief, but fortunately I found a marvelous therapist who assured me of my sanity.

Prior to all of this, I was what I have termed in my book, a "convenient Christian," believing only in as much as I felt was necessary *"just in case"* it was all true, and if there really was a place called "hell," I didn't want to go there (except to shake hands with all my friends, of course.) My logical mind developed early and I quickly doubted organized religion and a blind belief in the Bible as it was being taught. My church was similar to the Mormon (a spin-off) and very strict... but I could never "buy" the concept that ours was the only "true church."

To make a long story short, I began writing about my experiences as I continued to communicate with my angel guides and what resulted is my book, *Angels in My Life.* Although I knew/know my experience was not unique, until now I have not come *face to face* (so to speak) with anyone who has shared a like-experience. I think you can imagine my initial emotional reaction...in view of the doubt and negativity we face if we speak about our experiences.

When I saw on your Web site the title of your book and the cover with the picture of your beautiful son, I was stunned. The image of only head and shoulders was identical to the only part of Claricé that was before me in our initial communications. The trauma and emotional loss you and I both have suffered, there are no words adequate to explain. I always feared the loss of one of my four children and I never could have anticipated the pain of losing my wife, who was 13 years younger than myself.

I'll thank Russ Michael for referring me to you and will also write more again later after I "digest" the overall impact. Although the "confirmation" I received from our like-experiences was not necessary for my belief, it was still quite impactful.

Thank you much for sharing and may the angels continue to bless and guide you.

Victor Hosler
victorkh@verizon.net
St. Petersburg, Florida

Dear Suzy ....

Both of us have book-writing missions. My mission has been spelled out very clearly in that I am supposed to pass along the messages I receive for anyone who chooses to read them. Although I've learned that Clarice's and my time together was according to both of our life plans, the specific reason for her demise came about due to the problems in our HMO-dominated medical community and bottom-line oriented insurance companies and medical groups.

It was clearly shown to me that her death, in most circumstances, was medically unnecessary and thus was used as the cause, with the awareness that my anger over it would cause me to react and lead to my research into her medical records. That led to the book I've written with a working title of *20 Months to Diagnosis – 40 Days to Death.* I'm awaiting the resolution of the legal action that will hopefully draw media attention to the story whether we win or lose.

The manuscript clearly shows how women are being lied to and misled by doctors. They minimize the serious status of patients' diseases and don't give them the truth of the test results, much less actual copies that would permit looking into the meanings of the medical terminology — that certainly would lead to second and third opinions and demands for further diagnostics. It has been reported in the media that they are not doing proper diagnostics because the medical groups give bonuses for NOT doing them.

Yes, I would love to do the book trade you mentioned. I'll put *Angels in My Life* in the mail tomorrow. I believe we will both benefit down the road. I'm getting positive feedback from readers, some that are life-changing experiences.

I find it almost unbelievable that with the limited sales/distribution to date, that my writing has enhanced several lives, not to mention how it may affect others who witness the changes that have come about. Currently, along with my personal marketing efforts for *Angels,* I have begun a sequel, and I expect to use some of their stories in it.

This whole experience is just amazing to me. And the communications keep coming...my angels are always with me and guiding me on a daily basis.

Dear Suzy...

The books arrived and immediately into *Matthew, Tell Me about Heaven* I was "blown away"... almost like our phone calls and e-mails, I was literally almost in shock. Many of the questions I had regarding Claricé's communications with me were answered by Matthew's with you...and my jaw drops with each recognition of Matthew's words like those I've heard from Claricé.

As I go through the book, I highlight these similarities, and already many pages have highlighted passages and some pages have several. I am in so much awe, I had to share my feelings with you and as you know, I called while you were out and spoke with Bob before I retired for the night.

AND THEN IT BEGAN... What do you think?

Once in bed, I became restless and was tossing and turning just like I did in the earlier stages of the spiritual communications. I was getting new bits and pieces of information that didn't make sense. Finally, after about an hour, I decided to call upon Archie. *"Archie, could you bring Matthew Wade through to me?"*

His immediate answer was, *"I don't need to, Victor, he is here with us now. He knows you have been in communication with his mother. Let him come through to you."*

Then came Matthew:

"Hello Victor. I'm happy you are in communication with my mother. I believe you both will receive additional validation from your common experiences. I know you are both totally in belief of your experiences and neither one of you needs

validation, but still it comes now and will continue as you share what is happening in both your lives.

"You have expressed to my mother and Bob about your surprise at the depth of information I have given to her compared to the much simpler explanations and descriptions of Nirvana that you have gotten from Claricé." (Suzy, I must tell you that Matthew pronounced her name correctly, as it is in Portuguese. She was Brazilian and learned Portuguese even before her native Kamaiura Indian language.)

"The reason Claricé's information may have been more superficial is partly as you have mentioned to Bob and my mother — you would not have believed it if she had gone to the greater depths that I have gone into and would have rejected it because you were already in doubt in the beginning. Equally so, if she had gone where I have gone with my mother, you would have questioned it still further because it would have been beyond your Earthly experience of her communication abilities and technical knowledge.

"Claricé had to keep it simple to make you believe so that you would take on your new purpose in life. Even for this it was critical that she bring other entities to you to reinforce your belief in the communication you were having with her.

"Victor, if you want, keep reading the book about heaven, or Nirvana, really, as you, too, now know that is its proper name. But I would suggest that you set the other two books aside for now. They will only confuse you in trying to understand now what is not in the realm of your purpose in writing — it is much different from my mother's."

Suzy, then I asked Matthew, *"Do you mind if I call you Matt?"* And he said, *"I would prefer Matthew, but I do like the nickname 'Mash' that my mother often calls me because it momentarily takes me back to when we were together in body as well as spirit.*

"My mother is charged with writing about this universe and explaining the many, many aspects that go beyond the knowledge of those in your world about Nirvana and what the afterlife is all about with all of its nuances and complexities that those living on Earth have yet to learn and understand. There are many life forms in this universe with less, equal and greater intelligence than humans on Earth can conceive.

"You, Victor, have a different purpose. It is very important that you write about your wife's experience with the negligent medical community. But you misunderstood when you came to believe the cause of her demise was changed to a worldly need as it was getting near her time to leave you and the earthly plane. In truth, that experience of her illness was a part of her pre-birth agreement, because the awareness of the coming medical problems and need to remedy those was already known prior to her soul joining the seed within her mother's womb.

"Back to your purpose, which you already have begun with your writing and the experiences with others, it includes bringing enlightenment to your fellowman to look within for guidance from the Holy Spirit and all of the angels. This may be their soulmate or guardian angels who have made transition as well as those yet to make transition and who still will be available to assist them in their choices in life. Guidance is available also from other spiritual entities, often called spiritual guides or angel guides, who come forth from time to time as needed and requested.

"For every question mankind has, there is an answer if they would only ask and listen to 'the higher self within.' I like this reference you have used in the past. The recent and new words you are using, like 'observing the mind,' that you picked up from another enlightened soul, Eckert Tolle, in his book on the Power of NOW are excellent choices, too. When all of mankind learn to observe their minds as they take their daily walk, to ask for and listen to guidance and answers to their questions, all will begin to find more love and light of God, joy, happiness and harmony in their lives. This will spread throughout the world and peace may prevail.

"Victor, I want to assure you that Claricé will communicate with you again, perhaps in the near future to tell you about the work she is doing. As she told you, she is very busy teaching ...not just her painting and fine art, but she has a great sense of music and is teaching that as well. Also as she told you, she is working with the new souls who are about to be born...actually, re-born for the most part. Another of her focuses is teaching her love of the world's rainforests where she lived part-time as a child, the underwater and coral reefs she discovered when you worked in Mexico, and protecting the environment so that tomorrow's children will have a greater awareness of the need to protect and preserve the beauty of God's Earth.

"Claricé believes you are still too fragile for her to contact you at this time. But with the growth that is coming your way and spiritual understanding through your contact with my mother and others who may come to you due to your earlier communication with Russ Michael, I don't believe you will have to wait the fourteen years that my mother had to.

"As your Mexican friends would say, 'hasta luego.' Oh, one more note: You will learn more from the baby...you know what I mean, her interests and characteristics that already are stunningly similar to Claricé's. Your time in Mexico as a consultant was not just a position of employment. More and more meaning will follow over the next few years.

"Blessings to you, Victor."

Suzy, even though I typed that the following morning, I felt someone…surely Matthew…was giving me the words and refreshing my memory of the actual message the previous night. It "flowed out" as if being dictated to me.

Hi Suzy,

It is now a quarter to one in the morning and I was just driven from my bed by Archie. I went to bed at 11:30 p.m., rather calm compared to last night, and thought I would sleep easy and well. But, as I got near to drifting off, repeatedly I heard *"It's wrong Victor.... it's wrong."* My immediate reaction was the thought that my lower-self was trying to say my spirit communicating was wrong, that I shouldn't be doing this. Perhaps negative energy or the "evil influences" I've been accused of being involved with was wrong. I continued to ignore it and tried uselessly to get to sleep. Finally, a short time ago, I asked for Archie: *"Archie, I keep hearing the words 'it's wrong, it's wrong.' What is it? Who's telling me this and why?"*

Archie replied, *"I have been saying that to you since you began writing the message from Matthew at the computer, but you apparently were drained of energy and were ignoring me. What I was trying to tell you and am telling you now is that you asked for Matthew Wade, W-A-D-E, and that was wrong, even though we knew who you were asking for. Matthew's last name is Ward… W-A-R-D…."* As soon as he said that, I knew he was right because I remembered "Ward" from Russ Michael's review and newsletter as well as on your book and Web site. Then Archie said, *"When you began your writing, Matthew tried to correct you when you asked if you could call him Matt, but you didn't hear the difference in the sound of his last name and didn't think it was necessary to put it in that context and left it out."*

So much for telepathy. Even knowing he was right, I got up and looked at the book for reassurance and then to the e-mail I sent you and indeed it was wrong. Sorry, Suzy...Regards and blessings... Victor

Suzy...Thanks for the feedback regarding the Heaven Book...I had misunderstood Matthew. What he told you to tell me was right and I believe what he has given you will guide me. Very informative. I agree, little variations in what we receive is a matter of semantics...we "hear" information within our own frame of reference and our usual terminology to describe things and experiences.

[*Victor copied me on his lengthy e-mail to Russ Michael, which included Matthew's and Archie's transmissions, above, and the following similarity in Matthew's and Claricé's information.*]

Dear Russ,
Yesterday when Suzy's "Matthew Books" arrived, right away I dug into *Matthew, Tell Me about Heaven*. Immediately into the book, I was "blown away" and in awe of the messages she had received. I was literally almost in shock. Many of the questions I had regarding Claricé's communications with me were answered by Matthew's communications with his mother. The pieces of the puzzle that had mystified me from the beginning of my experience with Claricé's soul began to come together. MANY words and phrases were identical and/or too similar for this to be "accidental" or "coincidental."

One synchronicity I'll mention was especially interesting since I had questioned this when I had been told about it. Because there are so many belief systems and everyone comes to their own particular belief as to what heaven and the spiritual realm are, how could we all find what we believe that to be at the time of our passing or crossing over? Yet I was told that is what happens.

I haven't located the exact quote in my book yet, but my recall of it is, briefly: *What each one of humankind believes Heaven to be when they make their transition, is what they will find when they arrive in the spiritual realm, and they quickly realize the "wrongness" of their preconceived ideas.*

That is something I would never have looked for, or hoped to find, if I was searching for validation, but here is the quote from *Matthew, Tell Me about Heaven*:

There's another aspect of all this that I think you'll find interesting, Mother. When each person arrives, Nirvana is exactly what that individual imagined heaven to be during his Earth lifetime. The energy of the convictions within the individual's psyche creates for him the heaven of those convictions. Usually this is in great error!

DNA Repair

Dear Suzy,

After reading Matthew's message in Jean Hudon's compilation, I thought it might be appropriate to ask Matthew his opinion. I'd like to know if I am indeed repairing DNA damaged from Atlantean times and nuclear explosions and if that is a major part of my agreement to do this work now. I am afraid of "coming out."

I am an RN and alternative body-worker, but at the time I was first told that I could do this kind of work, I was not very aware of energetic healing or that I had an innate ability to do it. I felt compelled, partly by what I had been told and partly from within, to do something more than I had been. My hands began to move in the auric fields of the different people. It was as though I had dark material, sometimes it even felt metallic, in my hands. At the beginning, I had to do self-cleansings after each session. Gradually I learned to not take it on myself, to have it transformed immediately.

Since I wasn't trained to do this work, at least not in this lifetime, I questioned its validity in the beginning. But what almost always seemed to happen was that the people did get better. Basically, they seemed to connect more deeply to their own godselves and move forwards on their spiritual paths. I began to communicate with my "guides," most of whom seem to me to be other aspects of my greater being.

My husband has had difficulty accepting this particular kind of work (or it seems so to me). We were separated for nearly two years and when we got back together, I didn't start this work again. I didn't consciously realize that I was avoiding it, but I suppose I was/am afraid it will (again) cause problems in our relationship. However, I feel that I am not doing what I could be — this is an intuitive feeling — plus my energy has been more blocked since rejoining my husband than it had been in ages, possibly because I am not following my soul's calling, not in alignment with my purpose. In the last six months, I have been clearing, opening up my system again and the urge to go back to this work is becoming greater. On occasion, people do get to me for whatever reason and DNA repair happens during a session.

What I am getting to is that I still feel an inner drive to do this work, that I have some ability gained in former lifetimes to repair DNA. What I see in my sessions are metallic or golden threads feeding into the major 7 chakras. What I am getting or understanding is that these are the DNA threads that are not in the physical, but part of the soul that are torn and scattered. I don't know if there are many people who can do this repair. I do not want to feel special, that I can do something that others cannot. I sincerely want to serve humanity and if this is really a gift that I brought with me to share, I'd like to do so. I have stopped "advertising" or mentioning to others that I do this work, because I am not 100% certain that it is what it seems. Suzy, would you be so kind as to ask Matthew his thoughts on this.

Jamara

jamara@gmx.net

Dear Jamara, this is Matthew.

Thank you for writing to my mother, as if on cue from heavenly nudgings. You are recognizing your special gifts. To not recognize them would be, in the biblical quoting, "hiding your light under a bushel." Although you say you don't want to feel special, it is precisely this humility that lets me recognize you for the soul level healer you are.

I see you consciously and at soul level, and it is true that you do have this divine gift of healing DNA as well as lesser healing capabilities. That is, you are a total and true healer of body, mind and spirit on the level of lesser needs also, but your calling is the healing of the damaged DNA in souls who suffered this in eras of such destructiveness that Earth humankind cannot know its full measure. The souls who are led to you for healing are connected with you energetically far from Earth, for soul level connections of energy flow are not limited to communication just on the planet. The flow is coming from the stars, literally, as many of the souls led to you for this intricate repair are not of Earth. They are from within this galaxy, perhaps, and incarnated especially to receive the healing that you can do.

Please recognize that your longings to be using these rare gifts are not going to quiet themselves. This is your soul saying to you: *"We, your higher selves, have chosen this avenue, this healing pathway, from a sense of capability and desire, and you cannot deny this urgency to fulfill a mission that so few other mortals on Earth can do."* It is right to fully recognize consciously that this is your soul-level inclination, not only a consciously chosen mission, but something beyond your conscious knowing.

You are on a journey that is not meant to be unique only in the way you are thinking. *You yourself are unique.* You are not humankind like the masses on Earth, but of otherworldly life strains who chose to embody there during this unique time in the universe. You are there precisely to be doing the healing work you uncovered long years back, and this is what takes priority over all the other kinds of interests and talents you also possess.

Please let me speak a bit about the relationship with your husband. He has his own very special journey during this Earth incarnation. He, too, is from beyond Earth humankind. He has had more difficulty than you in relating to his soul-level calling and it is a frustration to him that he cannot identify this deep urging to break through a barrier resistant to the conscious connection. You chose to be together so that the gentleness of your understanding and patience along with sensitivity to him would give him the emotional climate for self-discovery. With that he would be propelled into his own soul's choice of light service during this era. He has succumbed to too much density in thoughts and feelings and has been too lax in pursuit of his soul's mission, and he is not providing the supportiveness to you that in the soul level agreement you and he made, he did willingly agree to do.

I am not in any position of star-level soul evolution discernment or authority or responsibility or desire to say that, since he has not progressed as he had freely and eagerly elected to do, and you have been sidetracked, so to speak, from your mission, it is not a necessity to remain in this union. Unions regarded on Earth insofar as legal and religious and even societal expectations of longevity are not regarded thus anywhere beyond your laws and moral codes. Choice to be in the flowing energy streamer as a union is within the pre-birth agreements, and if a union of souls is not meant to be a lifelong commitment designed to engender learning and soul growth, then it is not considered at soul level to be a requirement to remain together as partners.

Another sense in which the union also may be considered best dissolved is when one partner deters the other from progressing as the mission requires, and in this case, too, there is release freely granted by the two souls. Not consciously, you understand, but at soul level there is the awareness that when one or both partners have not adhered to the pre-birth agreement, there can be the need to dissolve the bond so that another attempt at the same mission, or lessons, can be undertaken. This can be an amended union arrangement that embraces another partner or it can be undertaken solely where the chosen mission can be fulfilled without a partner.

If you listen to your soul, you will choose whatever pathway will satisfy your deepest level urging. If you find it is distracting, frustrating, and even emotionally painful for you to stay in the union, then you would be hearing your soul's cries for its allowance to advance. If balance can be restored within your marital partnership, that surely can be regarded as fine, but if not, then the partnership can be dissolved for the highest good of both and permitting your healing mission to be resumed in full flower.

Jamara, please know that I do not willingly function in a role of marital counselor, and I am not now doing this. I am passing on your soul level cries to be heard, that balance and harmony are needed for your capability of healing to be realized most successfully. So, then, the union to remain or to be dissolved is a matter only for your conscious discernment and decision. Your light service is essential, either way. I send you evidence of the deep resonance of our souls in loving communion by telling you that there is a very special small animal that is in your utmost affection, and rightly so, as this dear small animal is a bit of energy from your own streamer.

With light to be shared with and shined upon your mission, this is Matthew.

Dear Suzy and Matthew,

I am so happy to hear from you. My life has taken several turns since our last correspondence. At first I was unable to break away completely from my husband, but I did begin doing more and more of my authentic work. Then I had three very telling dreams, knew we had to separate and wanted to do it in a good way. We separated in June and both of us are doing better. It is a very peaceful and friendly situation. I feel that he understands what is happening on a deeper level.

In February I fell (nearly fell off a cliff) and broke my arm and am still going to therapy for the countless "complications." What my injury and the complications have been doing is allowing me to integrate all of my parts, to strengthen myself on all levels. It has been trying at times, but when I look down at myself from a cosmic cloud and see the larger picture, I am very grateful. I know I have needed this time-out to be guided to my real purpose and I have gained a great deal of groundedness and inner discipline. What is wonderful is that a lot of unnecessary trauma that has been stored in my body since early childhood is also working itself out during this healing process.

Another big synchronistic event that I want to tell you about is, before I first wrote to you, I received a partial scholarship to a universal peace dance camp in beautiful Washington State. There I offered a worn-out new mother a healing session and she asked if I would work on her 7-month-old daughter. The session was amazing — it was craniosacral, energetic, a forgiveness session and bonding between mother and child. I had never worked on such a little child, neither energetically nor with craniosacral therapy.

When I returned to Switzerland my craniosacral teacher, a pediatrician, asked if he could put me on the list of therapists he wanted to personally recommend to work with babies and children. He asked me to take several specialized courses for craniosacral ostheopathy with babies and began sending children/babies to me immediately. Well...when I got Matthew's message, I had a feeling that some of the little ones came for special healing that the parents weren't aware of, and before each session I specifically asked for the energetic DNA healing to reach them simultaneously, if that was meant to be. Maybe you remember that Matthew told me that I had contacted you "as if on cue from heavenly nudgings"?

My healing sessions are becoming stronger and stronger, like in the old times. I love it—it brings me great joy. I can't tell you how exhilarated I am to have this reconnection. With love, blessings and joy to you both, Jamara

---

MATTHEW: The reference to DNA in Jamara's accounting is a soul's equivalent of a body's DNA—you have no word for that distinctive element of the soul—and the damage to souls' DNA that she spoke about is the most devastating in the universe. I am speaking only of souls, not physical or etheric bodies, because with one exception, the soul is not affected by the means its physical body is injured or dies. For instance, a disease-ravaged or a starved body causes no damage whatsoever to the soul and neither does a body that is blown to bits in battle or crushed in a vehicle crash. However, because the etheric body is so closely tied with the physical body, it is affected by traumatic experiences in the Earth lifetime or the dying process, and every person transitioning to Nirvana with a traumatized psyche receives instantaneous customized care and healing.

But here we are speaking only of the *soul,* and the one exception to its unchanged essence regardless of what happens to the body is the damage from nuclear detonations in space. Grievous damage due to warring in deep space was incurred by discarnate souls, those who were living in a free spirit state or were astrally traveling. Radioactive fallout from nuclear type explosions scattered those souls' parts, with each part at a loss to understand what had happened. The lengthy repair process requires specially trained teams to locate and retrieve all the parts and heal the various traumas they endured while separate from the rest of the soul; then they must be reintegrated so the fractured soul can be made whole again with all previous lifetime experiencing and knowledge intact.

Even though you cannot imagine the extent of complexities and time involved in the searching, healing and reintegrating, the very fact that the restoration process is undertaken lets you know the profound importance of each and every soul and the infinite love for all. That is why Creator made Its only exception to Its cosmic law that every soul's free will must be honored: *There will be no more nuclear detonations in space,* and It authorized the gods and goddesses who rule over their respective universes to prevent all free will attempts to start a nuclear war.

TO THE RESCUE

Dear Suzanne,

Could you please tell me if Matthew has spoken about Earthbound souls? And if he has, where can I obtain this information? Someone very dear to me has lost her 15-year old grandson. He committed suicide and is still here trying to communicate to the family. Please Suzanne, can you help me to help them?

Thank you and God Bless, Katherine

Dear Katherine...

I hope you have had time to read the books. The chapter "Suicide" in *Matthew, Tell Me about Heaven* might help ease the family's shock, grief and maybe guilt. "Astral Travel, Earthbound Souls" in *Illuminations for a New Era* describes the various types of souls who get caught between planes but not how to release them.

Matthew is suggesting that whoever notified the family the boy is trying to communicate with them explain to him that his family wants him to move into the light with their blessings—and tell the family they need to think and feel that. The boy's energy is still tied to theirs that is bound in pain, maybe guilt—they need to release those thoughts and feelings so only the love bonds remain—then the boy can move onward. I can relate to the family somewhat (not to their despair about the suicide) and understand that this could be more than they can handle right now. ....

Katherine, this was a new experience for me—in the past few minutes angels and Matthew and I helped the boy move through the light to Nirvana. The boy came to me and told me he is so so sorry that he did this, he didn't mean to kill himself, only wanted the attention and to show he was brave enough to try. His anguish was the pain he caused his family and also he felt that if he left the Earth plane, he would go to hell and be there forever. Please tell his family that he is being tenderly cared for in heaven, and he understands there is no punishment, that he'll have another chance for a lifetime where he won't do this again.

I don't know if his name is John—that name came to me and he said it was all right to call him that. My heart goes out to his family. I hope that reading the Heaven book will help them at least a little to cope with this.   Love, Suzy

Dear Suzanne,

To say thank you from the bottom of my heart does not seem sufficient for what you, Matthew and the Angels have done for this family. I did not even expect a response from you personally. Your response just blew me away. Just so you know, you are correct about the boy's name, it's spelled Jon. That was the validation the family needed. Thank you for that. I have given my friend a copy of *Matthew, Tell Me about Heaven*. I know it will be read by many of the family members. I have thanked Matthew and the Angels and one more time I would like to thank you dear dear kindred spirit. Peace, Light and Love always. Katherine

Dear Suzanne,

I forwarded your e-mail response to me about my friend's grandson Jon to her and she read it to her son, the boy's father. He did find much comfort in what you said. So much so, and this is what I really want to tell you, he mentioned it to a man he works with whose wife has crossed over recently. This man asked if he could read the e-mail, which he did. He has also found great comfort in your words that seemingly weren't intended for him. Or were they? I thought you would like to hear about this.

Peace, Light and Love, Katherine

Dear Katherine...

My experience with Jon was a first for me, and I wrote you while I was still in awe. To tell you more, when I was asking God to send him help, suddenly a boy's face filled my "mind's eye" and that's when the name John—Jon— came to me. He talked with me a lot, what he'd done and his anguish about it, he was so very sorry about the pain it caused his family, his fear that if he left the Earth plane, he'd be doomed to hell for eternity. He was very afraid when the first two angels appeared—he said the devil disguises itself as angels and he didn't want them to come near him because they would carry him to hell.

I asked him if he trusted me. He said he did and I talked with him about my trust in the angels and asked him to let them come close enough so he could feel their presence and to tell me how he felt then. He agreed and when the angels slowly went nearer, he told me they felt warm and loving—that calmed him. I knew Matthew was with me, and I told Jon about him and about life in heaven, including no punishment and a chance to not repeat what he had done. Matthew told Jon that he and the angels would go with him to heaven, he didn't have to go alone, then the image in my mind was of Jon and the two angels gently floating into the light and many angels in the distance joining them. Matthew told me that Jon was greeted lovingly and being tenderly nurtured.

Last night Jon came back to me and thanked me for helping him. He said he was so happy to be in that beautiful place, that his life there is wonderful and to please let his family know. So even if I hadn't heard from you today, I would have written to give you that extra information to pass on to Jon's family.

When I read this e-mail from you, my reaction was "No, that was only for Jon." Immediately Matthew told me that what happened went way beyond that. Jon's experience was a catalyst for 1000s of trapped souls to be released from whatever had kept them Earthbound—often this is not realizing they've left their Earth bodies, but it also can be that their family's intense grief holds them here or they have remorse like Jon felt. I don't know if the wife of the man you wrote about was ever Earthbound, but since he felt comforted by what I wrote about Jon even though it wasn't meant for him, and especially because of those far-reaching effects that Matthew told me about—that may indeed have been a message from his wife's soul to his soul and he received it intuitively.

I'm so very grateful for that unique experience of being able to help in the way I did.   With blessings and LOVE and PEACE...Suzy

PART IV

MORE FROM MATTHEW

MESSAGE FOR WESAK

Matthew was invited to be a presenter at the May 2003 WESAK, an annual three-day spiritual celebration held in Mt. Shasta, California. Since I am not a "live channel," shortly before Bob and I left, Matthew gave me a half-hour message to read. The original book contained his full message; some of it is tucked into new chapters in this edition or similar information is given by other sources. Part of the excerpts below were selected to show Matthew's emphasis on love-light in the message and the rest provide information that isn't in the three earlier books.

We speak of "light beings" and "light workers" and "light service," but we could just as correctly say "love" because love and light are not separate powers. The total essence of Creator is love, and it is expressed in the obvious, tangible, directional ways that light can be used and observed, just as love is easily seen in its manifestations.

The capacity to love is your birthright. It is the composition of your soul. Because Creator is the supreme being of the cosmos, and God — by that name and others — is the Supreme Being in our universe, each of us is a part of Creator via God. Thus all of us are inseparably connected through their love essence and each of you has the innate ability to shower love upon your planet and every other soul living there.

The all-powerful eternal unity of love and light is the

healing force of your world. Indeed, it is the ONLY force that can heal the pain felt by Earth and her people and all of her other life forms. The universal law is as simple as each soul feeling, receiving and sending the energy that we call love or light.

The struggle between the darkness and the light will continue only until these opposite perspectives are reconciled and Earth's balance is regained. This is happening! …. Your invaluable help in bringing this about is by sending love to all of Earth's people, especially to those who are *causing* the suffering. This is the ONLY way *all* suffering can end there! My mother said that she can't sincerely send love to people who are doing things she abhors, and I'll tell you exactly what I told her, because it may serve you well, too:

Mother, you would turn on a flashlight to guide someone out of the darkness of uncertainty and anxiety onto a path where they are confident and secure, wouldn't you? Those souls have lost their way and are fearful and foundering. Do not think of them as their deeds, but rather what you want for the world. Think of kindness, helpfulness and justness and sharing, think about the world's people living in harmony, peacefulness and love, and send those thoughts to those souls in darkness.

Your planet has been ascending into fourth density for some time, but in some minds there is a misunderstanding about this. There will not be two planets Earth, as some have theorized, one that stays in third density to support those who are resistant to the light and one that ascends with all her light-receptive souls. Earth is one soul, not two, and she has chosen to journey into a higher, then higher frequency.

It is true that highly evolved people have been thriving

happily and graciously in Earth's interior for ages; however, they are not physical survivors of the ages of Atlantis and Lemuria. They arrived when the planet was still in a recovery mode from the cataclysmic explosions of those continents, when all life was lost. At the point when Earth was considered habitable, repopulating was once again undertaken by the same ancestors of the original Earth human population. The first contingent that arrived found living much more hospitable underground as the planet's surface had not reached a point of recovery for comfortable living. Due to their spirituality level, those souls retained knowledge of their beginnings; however, the limitations of Earth's third density could affect accurate memories of all their subsequent experiencing.

Knowing of [Earth's Golden Age] sustains your faith that *love is creating* these glories for Earth! It's also important for you to know that the various misconceptions I've mentioned — and any other differing views about your planetary history and current events — are all right! As long as the Christed light is guiding your pathway, it isn't necessary that everyone believe exactly the same!

A smile is the easiest way to spread love and light and healing. The ripple effects of just one heartfelt smile are incalculable!

LIGHTWORKERS

Something that isn't known to the extent it needs to be is the ever-increasing numbers of lightworkers. Millions of people are participating in international meditations, prayer services and rallies for peaceful changes. Individuals and groups are actively helping people in distant lands or are financially supporting organizations engaged in those efforts. Others are involved in community assistance programs, and some folks with "celebrity" status are spearheading movements that are growing in effectiveness. Multitudes all over the globe are working toward the betterment of their communities, their countries, their world. Relatively few of those many millions think of themselves as the lightworkers they are or realize that the radiant light generated by their unity in spirit, unity in compassion, caring and sharing—unity in godly service— is raising vibrations throughout Earth and increasing her ascension momentum.

It is not only for "kindred spirit" reinforcement that you who *know* you are lightworkers need to be aware of that collective light power, but also as encouragement to beam your light beyond your circles of like-minded souls. The vast majority of peoples have no idea whatsoever that the planet is fast leaving third density. Even with all their efforts to improve conditions, they see the continuance of war, violence and injustice, impoverishment and environmental destruction, and they despair: What kind of world is that for their children and grandchildren to inherit?

You can reduce, perhaps even eliminate, the negativity of despair in those individuals by *living your light*. I don't mean preaching or proselytizing, I mean living with such glowing spirit that it permeates everyone near you. When they ask how you can feel such optimism, confidence and joy, offer as much of your enlightenment as they are comfortable hearing.

Please don't think, however, that you should keep your knowledge under a bushel, so to say. You know family members, friends, neighbors and colleagues who are reluctant to accept whatever doesn't fit into their ideas and beliefs—respect that, knowing that they will have other opportunities to "see the light." For soul-searchers, though, having someone with whom to share your intuitions and convictions can be immensely reinforcing, so when open-minded individuals indicate that they would welcome a discussion, offer as much as they are comfortable hearing. If they seem somewhat skeptical, still you have planted a seed that could grow into full blossom. With the light on Earth more intense than any of you can consciously remember, minds are opening just as hearts are.

So let your light shine in all its glory—it is a most meaningful, fulfilling life mission.

THE IMPORTANCE OF LOOKING FORWARD

Matthew was asked his opinion of the proposed prayer to be used as a global request for an individual's protection.

My thoughts are that the prayer for that person's protection needs to be expanded to all whose courage and perseverance have exposed the truth of what has been perpetrated upon Earth, with the prayer participants expressing love and gratitude for everyone whose efforts are bringing the darkness to light. Without the service of these brave souls who are discovering and publicizing dark activities, those would stay hidden and continue to cause injustices and suffering.

So it is essential that people be truthfully informed so they can demand reforms that will end the misery caused by those activities, and it is just as necessary for them to put the energy of their thoughts into manifesting still more light on the planet. Focusing intently on what is past and still is happening gives power to the darkness behind it, whereas a collective vision and action toward a world of love, truth and harmony will help bring that about more quickly.

It is far more advantageous to cease preoccupation with the darkness and shift thoughts to "seeing" the world as you want it to be. The more energy put forth in looking forward with optimism, the more swiftly and surely reforms will occur. That kind of focus adds to the love-light that is enabling spiritual renewal worldwide and disabling the remaining pockets of darkness. That would be a far more appropriate and loving tribute to that courageous individual and all other brave souls whose service so greatly is helping to enlighten the public and by so doing, uplift Earth herself.

TELEPATHIC COMMUNICATION, DISCERNMENT

Telepathic communication is not what many regard it, a unique gift that very few people have. *Every one of you* has the capacity for that soul-to-soul communion as your birthright—it is an ingredient of your soul. With the higher frequencies prevailing on Earth, connections are opening quite rapidly; however, do not be discouraged if yours has not. It will when the time for you is right, but a sense of urgency to communicate with a loved one in Nirvana, for instance, can create an energy barrier and delay your connecting. And you must be mindful that not only light beings—your beloved souls in spirit or ascended masters or members of spiritually advanced physical civilizations —want to talk with you; dark entities are just as eager to reach you with their DISinformation. To keep away the latter, simply ask to be protected by the Christed light and demand that only light beings may contact you.

Although asking and receiving is just that easy, you must act responsibly. If you are feeling tired or ill or beset with worries about anyone or anything—any type of stressful condition—do NOT attempt a telepathic connection; to do so would be an invitation to low entities because your energy level is too low to reach the high vibrations of light beings. Feeling egotistical about your achievement is a certainty that you will reach low-level beings as egotism carries an energy attachment that is incompatible with light, whereas humility and thankfulness are light vibrations.

The explosion of the "information age" has inundated your world with reading material, and being discerning about what is the truth and what is not is essential not only to be accurately informed, but developing discernment is a step in spiritual evolvement. The Internet has enabled swift and wide dissemination of accurate information that previously was known by only a comparative handful; and although it is the best source of myriad factual reports, it is equally useful to the dark ones on and off-planet to promote their agenda.

Material purported to be a transmission from a high light being actually may have been written in offices right on the planet to give *dis*information amidst familiar spiritual words. Some receivers are unaware that they are reaching base entities that claim they are a well known, respected light source and give false information; those receivers unwittingly distribute the falsehoods that may be accompanied by some valid information to beguile readers into thinking the entire message is truthful.

Some messages are filled with gloom and doom, such as mammoth changes in seas and landmasses will require your evacuation by ETs and when you return to the planet, you'll have to live underground. That is pure nonsense. What is true is that more geophysical happenings are ahead as the negativity is lifted and dispersed or transmuted into light, and your space family's technology will continue reducing the disastrous effects of the events while permitting the same amount of negativity to be released.

Be discerning about *all* information by asking within, connecting consciously with your soul, wherein the truth lies. If the information flows with ease, it is aligned with your soul's truth; if you experience a jolting or resistance sensation, it is not. More so than at any other time in the last two millennia, in this time of ever-intensifying light, consciousness-soul connections are easier. However, if a mind is closed to all information except that which dovetails with rigid beliefs, the soul's messages can't penetrate that barrier.

Every one of you is beloved by all souls in higher realms, and we fervently wish that you would not approach life as if it were a complex and mysterious endurance test. Far from that, life is as simple as letting love be your guide, your understanding and your fulfillment.

ELDERLY WITH DEMENTIA

With the "baby boomers" in their 60s, Alzheimer's is looming as a major concern of your medical establishment—indeed, society itself. Like many other projections that are based on unawareness of Earth's ascension, within a short time dementia of any sort will not be an issue in your world. As Earth continues her ascension into higher vibratory planes, people receptive to the light that is continuously intensifying will physically travel with her into the lighter density. The absorption of light not only enables survival in the higher vibrations, it changes the cellular patterning into a crystalline form that doesn't degenerate like third density body cells do. Mental disorders and all other kinds of physical maladies now rampant on Earth will be incrementally cured as the planet reaches higher and higher frequencies.

In addition to that assurance, I want to speak about something that cannot be known to any of you: What karma is underlying persons afflicted with dementia? And there is no one response because each situation is as individual as each soul is, but there are a number of possibilities to consider.

In cases where the caretaking is with love and patience, the people are reflecting the peacefulness of the soul. There *is* soul awareness, of course, but no conscious thinking that families and caretakers would consider sensible. This period of what appears to others as irrationality, perhaps, may be the soul's reward, we could say, for having experienced severe traumas during the current lifetime, and the respectful, diligent nurturing is healing them psychically now instead of waiting for that healing in Nirvana. Or they may be achieving the same kind of karmic balancing after having been mistreated in one or more previous lifetimes.

When there is no kindness or conscientiousness in the treatment of these elderly, karma also may be playing itself out. They may have chosen to serve as the lesson-givers for the souls in charge of their care, offering them the opportunity to balance traumas in previous lives where they were neglected or scorned or terribly mistreated; that could have been a lifetime that brought dementia with aging, or they simply were old and feeble and treated as a burden on the family. While this may be the very same souls in role reversals, that isn't a requirement—all pre-birth agreements are designed for spiritual growth of all the principals sharing the lifetime and all agreements are made in unconditional love.

The elderly we're speaking of may be achieving their own balance, having in another lifetime caused misery for old folks in their care. Or they may be reaping what they sowed during this lifetime that was far afield of their souls' choices, and if so, this could be a case of divine grace—their souls may have petitioned for a contract amendment that offered the opportunity to achieve balance during the incarnation by absorbing sufficient light to make the physical journey with Earth into fourth density's higher vibrations. Even if physical death comes prior to that time, the souls would be at that light status in the spirit world because they had completed all their third density karmic lessons during the Earth lifetime.

Many millions of souls are living in much harsher circumstances than chosen in their contracts, and they petition for an amendment to leave the lifetime sooner than they originally chose. When this is a mass petition—many souls in the same area requesting the same thing—often they leave about the same time, perhaps in a disease epidemic or an environmental disaster or in civil wars or starvation in lands of famine. But by and large, elderly persons with dementia are living out their chosen karmic experiencing, whether by original or amended soul contract, and most likely their caretakers are too.

ABOUT THOSE ETs ON EARTH

The dark minds need to concoct something dramatic to again unite you all in fear, and it could be their plan for an alien invasion. This isn't a new idea—it has long been in some governments' top secret military contingency and strategy plans, but not intended to be used unless the population started strongly resisting being controlled. And you are! More than ever before, you are embracing compassion and kindness, caring and sharing, and many in oppressed nations are calling for freedom. All of these feelings and actions are increasing light on Earth and making it more and more difficult for those in the camp of the darkness to keep a cover on their deception, corruption and brutality. So they may be motivated to unveil the *underground* extraterrestrials as a means to keep alive the Illuminati intent to enslave the world through fear.

Their purpose of inciting fear is twofold. Energy with fear attachments is anathema to the energy of light, and light absorption is essential for both spiritual clarity and cellular restructuring so bodies can survive in the higher light densities into which Earth is ascending. Second, the controlling forces do NOT want light to expose their dark deeds, and creating mass fear has been an effective means of preventing that. But it isn't working well any longer— our space family keeps preventing the success of "black ops" terrorism—and in their desperation to hold onto their ebbing control, the dark minds need some dynamic measure to fill the populace with fear. That is why they may try to send the underground alien population to the surface to "invade." If so, it won't work. Those aliens, commonly called "Little Greys," won't unite to participate in such a devious plan, and in conjunction with light beings living among you, they will thwart any attempt to pull it off.

When they arrived 60 to 70 years ago, they didn't expect to be trapped in Earth's atmosphere, but they were, and ever since then they have been largely unseen residents. They came to offer their advanced technologies in exchange for conducting experiments with the Earth humans with whom they had soul contracts for enhancing the emotional aspects of their species.

They were betrayed. There was a futile attempt to annihilate them after they shared their technologies, which included weather control and space craft designs; abduction stories were fabricated even as they were denounced as hoaxes while true accounts of the Greys' gentleness in the experiments were suppressed; cattle mutilations were blamed on them; and their appearance was depicted with words designed to be frightening. Although these people do look different from you, they are a human civilization and, like you, some have lower light frequency than others. A few of those lower light beings ignored the soul-level agreement specification that experiments could be conducted *only* if the Earth individuals had conscious memory of the agreement, and dreadful fear and suffering were caused to the persons who did not remember.

But as a group, the Greys who have been residing on Earth for many decades have no more desire to harm you, much less take over your world, than do the many millions of *bona fide* extraterrestrials who have been assisting you in myriad ways. The Illuminati know the truth about the presence and purpose of all these civilizations, and they know that *none* poses an iota of danger to you! Totally to the contrary, the danger posed to your world is the Illuminati itself and its struggle to continue controlling life on Earth. Your universal family has been helping you to insure that that struggle is in vain.

In addition to the powerful civilizations that are beaming their intense light from vast distances, approximately 17 major groups of extraterrestrial forces in nearer civilizations are working on your behalf. The numbers vary in accordance with Earth's needs being accomplished or remaining, and at this time the largest contingent is from Arcturus, the next is from Lyra—both were the original homelands of some of Earth's earliest settlers. Forces from the Pleiades are not the largest in members, but they have the most potent technology for clearing the lower atmosphere and reducing the destructive effects of geophysical occurrences. Andromedans and Sirians also have been active, often in cooperation with other groups that have experience in life-preserving services in many galaxies. Many of you have ancestors from one or another of those civilizations.

Although the great majority of your nearby helpers are in spacecraft surrounding Earth, some are living right there among you. In their homelands some civilizations may not have shapes and features similar to yours, but their manifesting capabilities permit them to make bodies that fit in with the population wherever they are. And, appearing just like you, they are able to attain influential positions because of their extraordinary intelligence. Their brains are not as constrained by third density limitations as are Earth human brains, and they can see beyond your vision and hear beyond your hearing. Some are born to Earth parents, others simply show up with standard documents regarding birthplace, education, work experience and the like. Once they are seen as risks to Illuminati objectives, their highly developed psychic abilities alert them to dangerous situations and they can manifest protective shields or disappear by dematerializing. When it is safe to do so, they will reveal themselves for who they really are, and when love and peace reign completely on Earth, they may choose to continue to help you if invited or return to their own worlds.

However, not all extraterrestrials who have been interfacing with Earth are benevolent. Some civilizations, primarily the reptilians, have been wreaking havoc on the planet for eons. But it wouldn't matter what civilization the dark forces infiltrated to spread their agenda, the light forces, which have no civilization boundaries either and whose only weapon and defense is light, are by far the most powerful warriors in this universe. The influence of the reptilians and others of dark proclivity in your galaxy is waning, and light-filled reptilians are helping in this triumph for the light.

At soul level, every person in every civilization throughout this universe is inseparable from all others — whether within the light or within the darkness, primitive or highly evolved, beautiful or ugly by your standards, every one is a part of God and comprises the Oneness of All.

WHAT'S GOING ON IN
THE SOLAR SYSTEM

Suzy: Some scientists are concerned about the increase in the sun's coronal activity and its long-term effects on the planet. So, tell me what's going on in the solar system.

MATTHEW: Your scientists are viewing the accelerated activity insofar as their scientific equipment and analyses can, but it surely is not the whole picture or the correct one. Simply, your solar system is reflecting the stepped-up activity in the galaxy, which is reflecting the same in the universe, so this is a monumental chain reaction and your astronomers are observing only a minute part of it.

Mother, since you don't have any scientific knowledge or scientists' hesitation to accept information that differs from their theories, your idea that this is simply an effect of the intensifying light is much more accurate than theirs. That is basically what is happening, and the effects upon your planet are totally beneficial. This solar activity is dislodging and reducing or eliminating the heaviest pockets of negativity still remaining above, on and within the planet, and Earth has been releasing it via earthquakes, volcanic activity and violent storms. While much of this activity has been manmade, using weather control technology to cause death, devastation and fear that creates more negativity, the results nevertheless are benefiting the planet. Earth would be quaking and erupting anyway, but with care to minimize the death toll and destruction. When the events are manmade, extraterrestrial technology distributes the released energy currents to greatly lessen the effects.

Why were there isolated catastrophes like Krakatau, Mt. Vesuvius and the flood that God told Noah to prepare for?

For the same reason that similar things are happening now. Without the ET technology's ameliorating power, you would see the same severity. Even as recently as twenty-some years ago, when there wasn't enough light on the planet to transmute the negativity into light, it was thought that planetary cleansing would require serious geographic alterations.

And Mother, "Noah's flood" did not cover the entire planet — many high areas were not flooded and the populations there also survived — and those volcanic eruptions were not as isolated as you think. Many others as well as earthquakes occurred in susceptible places around those same times to release pent up negativity. A beneficial but temporary treatment, you could say, as none of that activity could cure negativity's cause: the darkness in humankind. This time, Earth is going for the *cure* — she's leaving third density, where darkness abounds.

Good for her and us! Can the sun's increased activity cause any environmental or atmospheric damage?

That activity is *repairing* the damage that has been caused by negativity! The greater the polarity between positive and negative vibrations on Earth — or more simply stated for this purpose, "good" and "bad" behavior — the greater the corresponding extremes in climate. The depth and breadth of ice in your polar zones did not always exist, nor did the repressive heat and humidity of the equatorial regions. Vast desert areas didn't exist either, nor did violent storms. All of *that* is the damage!

As Earth rises into still higher vibrations, there will be a gradual reversal of all that damage and the more recent environmental destruction. Eventually there will be a temperate climate worldwide, deserts will become fertile lands where life can once again flourish; and even though the polar regions will melt, the cold temperatures of seas that marine life requires to thrive will be stabilized as the pollution is removed from your water and air. Earth's planetary body will be restored to the purity and beauty of the paradise it was in the beginning days.

February 1, 2011

Matthew, what about the shifting of Earth's magnetic pole that has some people worried about what that portends?

The worries are needless, Mother. The shift is a corrective action that began 60 to 70 years ago, when the planet was so deeply mired in third density's negativity that its orbit had become seriously unsteady. Without the help of powerful distant sources that infused Earth with light to start stabilizing her orbit, the planet would have flown out into space and certain destruction.

It's understandable that your scientists don't know how to account for the increase in solar flares or the pole shift or why so many strange celestial bodies are appearing. All of these are perfectly natural along Earth's ascension route, which has taken her far, far beyond her former neighborhood, and your scientists think she's still in that space that's familiar to them.

Well, that makes sense! How much of the recent monumental snowstorms and major flooding in many countries is manmade?

It isn't an exaggeration to say "all of it." The Illuminati's technologists don't have to initiate each incident—once elements in the atmosphere have been set in motion, the domino effect takes over and a strong storm begets a slightly weaker one, that one sets off another and so it goes. When conditions start easing as the energy within them dissipates, the weather manipulators set off another disruption. It's the same with volcanic eruptions and earthquakes—once that tremendous energy is moving, it hops from one place to another where Earth's crust already is weakened.

If one isn't aware of the Illuminati and their objectives, it's logical to ask, *Why are they manipulating weather and creating natural disasters?* The answer is, to produce the negativity that arises out of fear, chaos, widespread destruction, economic disasters and general misery. Take heart in knowing that they can't keep at this much longer because *nothing* with dark intent can exist in the intensive light of Earth's Golden Age.

AND MORE...

The following are excerpts from Matthew's recent messages.

If you remembered all your soul contract provisions, what purpose would the physical lifetime serve? What advancement could there be in spiritual clarity, application of universal laws and use of free will if you simply followed decisions you made before knowing what circumstances you would encounter during the lifetime?

Forgetfulness of soul contracts, which cover the foundation and major players that fit the soul's chosen experiencing and let the personage fill in the details as life keeps unfolding, isn't meant to drown anyone in a lifelong sea of confusion, and it doesn't if folks pay attention to their soul level guidance that is as unmistakable as gigantic flashing arrows. Following those bright blinkers that are conscience, intuition, inspiration, instinct and so forth, aligns conscious decisions with contract choices.

However, that does not negate your free will to deviate from the contract when other opportunities for growth arise. Contracts aren't rigid, but rather allow for flexibility as different kinds of situations can offer the same measure of learning—actually, it isn't learning, it is *remembering what your soul knows.* Spiritual growth is a series of self-discoveries that get passed on from lifetime to lifetime, and each contract is designed to provide opportunities for the soul to keep evolving.

Awareness of a "mission" — a term that denotes a soul's primary purpose for embodying — doesn't pop up as an *Aha!* moment, it comes as meaningful accomplishments that impart a sense of fulfillment. And no lifetime ever is wasted! What you consider "mistakes" because they lead to situations that are very difficult to handle are not a waste if you learn from them. Furthermore, they may be part of your contract — not all lifetimes can be on Easy Street or there could be no advancement for the soul. Evolvement requires balance, and attaining balance requires dealing with stressful situations as well as enjoying ideal circumstances. Incarnating offers myriad possibilities and probabilities, but no certainties that would preclude your making the many choices that let each lifetime become a unique learning adventure.

God explained this more succinctly in His reply to my mother when she asked why people can't know everything that their souls know:

If all were absolutely known, if nothing required any independent thinking or decisions or activity, then why would there be any need for multiple experiencing? What would there be to learn? Why would life itself be necessary? We could just fast forward to The End, which is The Beginning, and let all lives of all times reside at that initial point of Being.

The shooting in Tucson, Arizona, was as reported, a mentally unstable young man's attempt to kill Congresswoman Giffords and as many of her supporters as he could, but it was not the "senseless act" as often described. The shooter was acting under mind control and all who were killed or wounded either followed original soul contracts wherein they had chosen to participate in an event with "a higher purpose" or just prior to the shooting, they amended their contracts to include that incident for that same purpose.

While it was unquestionably traumatic on a conscious level for those who were wounded and their families, and a tragedy for all who loved the persons who were killed, at soul level the participants willingly served to force attention on the inevitable results of increasingly vitriolic rhetoric in a society that has become inured to that kind of speech as well as violence. This pervasive conditioning had to be brought to the forefront of national, *international*, awareness so the outcry for an end to incivility and violence can change the collective consciousness of your civilization, which in large part has accepted that kind of behavior as an innate aspect of human nature.

That behavior is NOT an innate aspect of human nature—it is *taught!* The makeup of souls is pure light, which is the same as love, and it is the most powerful force in the universe. Violence, divisiveness and hatred are deliberately introduced through the many influences that impact life on Earth. And because whatever constitutes your collective consciousness is what creates your world, it is essential that those influences *be brought to light* so healing and unified spirit can be the legacy not only of the lives affected by the shooting in Tucson, but the lives of all souls who have helped to cleanse your world of darkness. Not punishment or revenge or retaliation will ever bring peace and harmony—only LOVE can end the illusion of separateness and let the innocence and purity of infants reenter hearts and minds.

Light beings throughout the universe honor the souls who agreed to be "victims" in Tucson. Those who died were lovingly, gratefully greeted in Nirvana, light is being intensely beamed to their grieving families and friends, and those who are recovering from wounds have angelic helpers assisting the medical teams. However, do not for a moment underestimate the relevancy and power of untold numbers of prayers and heartfelt sentiments in those respects!

US President Obama's memorial address was transmitted to us from Earth's monitors in Nirvana. We know the soul of this man, thus better than he knows himself, yet without his conscious awareness that he willingly left his spiritually advanced civilization to serve in the vanguard of the Golden Age master plan, his words on that memorial occasion were from his heart and soul in concert with all the heavenly hosts.

We are joyous for the triumphant Egyptians, just as we are for the citizens of Tunisia, and shall be for people in all countries where voices for freedom are raised in unison and peacefulness. The past weeks' incidents are clear evidence that the light is permeating the collective consciousness as your world is seeing the power of people who are unified in purpose. In Earth's field of potential, the unstoppable momentum of this exhilarating energy is hastening the day when your world is free from every form of suppression, oppression and deprivation.

Along the way, as everything in the universe keeps speeding up, heads will be spinning as significant happenings come one after another, or, more likely, simultaneously. Seeing their tattered remnants of influence coming to an end, the Illuminati will try to convince the populace that the truths that are forthcoming are outrageous, and their unwitting allies will be those who will resist having their firm beliefs upended. For example, the origin of Earth's civilization. The staunch believers in evolution and the equally adamant believers in grand design: How easily will they accept the truth that both sides are partly right, partly wrong? And how much more difficult will it be for the religiously devout when the truth emerges about the purpose of religions and the falsehoods that are the foundation of Christianity?

It will be traumatic for many when those revelations and others come forth at the same time major changes are being introduced. Knowing that all of the confusion and turmoil is heralding Earth's exit from third density, you lightworkers are ideally prepared to weather the coming months and to help those who are foundering.

———————————

A concern in many minds is the mysterious sudden deaths of millions of birds and fish in various locations around the globe. This was not from a single cause, but a "last straw." The small bodies of those animals are more vulnerable than human bodies to the many forms of toxic pollutants in your air, water and soil, so their immune systems were seriously weakened before they were hit by a blast of low vibrations from manmade electromagnetic grids.

If you are wondering why our space family did not use their technology to prevent such a blast, it is because doing so exceeds their authority. They are, however, permitted to deflect or neutralize harmful radio waves aimed at the peoples, and they did so; without their intervention, there would have been many human bodies sickened or killed along with the mass exodus of birds and fish.

———————————

The teeter-tottering of the international economy cannot be sustained much longer, nor can the history of its control by the Illuminati's illegal manipulations remain hidden much longer. They are using obscure legal processes to hold onto their ill-gotten fortunes, thus we cannot tell you when the economic collapse will come. However, the time cannot be far off because many nations are bankrupt or on the verge, and their leaders and economists know that there is no financial backing for the daily computer transactions in the trillions of dollars and other currencies. When the collapse does come, welcome it in the knowledge that those who will direct the new system are at the ready and during the transition will keep financial disruptions to a minimum. You can lessen the anxiety of those around you by remaining postive, and you can do that confidently, knowing that Earth's Golden Age is right around the corner, so to say.

Please do not be dismayed because attempts to manifest strong healthy bodies or high energy levels haven't produced desired results. Third density powers of manifestation are not sufficiently developed so that a weak body can be transformed into glowing health or a low energy level raised to high in the twinkling of an eye. But by all means, continue to "see" yourselves in those prime states— positive thoughts about well being attract the energy of similar thought forms in the universal soup and enhance your chances of success. As Earth's ascension journey continues, the higher vibrations will improve health conditions and strengthen your abilities to manifest along with your *belief* that you do indeed have that power.

Some have expressed concern that feeling heaviness of heart about world affairs will dim their light to the extent that they won't be able to live in fourth density vibrations. It is natural to feel compassion for all who are suffering—people, animals, Mother Earth herself—and while that emotion can make a heart feel heavy, within compassion there is light. Self-pity is quite another thing, however, so do not fall into that dark trap. To lighten heavy hearts, send forth healing light to all the world; remember that millions who are suffering are completing chosen karmic experiencing; feel grateful, not guilty, for all the blessings in your lives; and visualize Earth's Golden Age where only peace, love, cooperation and joy exist—that world is coming closer and closer!

———————————

As for the onset of the Golden Age, not all of its glories are sitting on its doorstep, so to say. Yes, everything born of dark intent will have ceased with the advent of that Age—so no more warring or other violence, no more impoverishment or disease, no more polluting or mind control or corruption. All necessary truths will have been revealed and there will be reformed governments and economic, legal and judicial, energy, educational, communication and transportation systems. That is but a partial list of great changes underway, and at the end of 2012, none of them can be considered as perfected. Refinements will continue in all of those areas and other advancements too, and as you keep growing spiritually and intellectually, you will greet all forward strides with rejoicing.

PART V

OTHER VOICES
BEYOND EARTH

ASCENDED MASTERS

Hatonn

Suzy: I keep forgetting to ask God if Metatron is the name of the part of Him that people hear, so I'm asking you — is it?

HATONN: Aren't you embarrassed to ask about something you really *do* know, Suzy? Why would God give his voice a special name? Did He ever ask you to address Him as Metatron?

No, but some people believe that Metatron is the speaking part of God.

They're wrong. They're just putting another unnecessary layer between their conscious selves and their godselves. And like every other soul in this universe that is its own unique soul-self with its own voice, Metatron is his own unique soul-self with his own voice .

What about the other ascended masters? Is the information about them being taught accurately?

Suzy, most of them are APPALLED at much that is being taught about them! If anyone knows how faulty the idea is that they must be called upon to guide and instruct on the pathway to God, it is *they themselves!* At Matthew's evolved state, he ranks with the "ascended masters" but he doesn't consider himself this and for good reason—the souls who are given those exalted designations *don't* ascribe them to themselves!

Like all other souls, each of them has a name, a soul mission, the destination of reintegration with God and Creator, and its own soul pathway to discover on the journey, and they're doing it just as you are—connecting directly with God. You know that the layers of church hierarchy were intentionally established to distance God from souls. Can't you see that this "ascended masters" designation has exactly the same effect, but perhaps with loftier motives?

I hadn't thought of that comparison. But isn't it true that they are much higher in the light than the vast majority of souls and they have a "divine" status that we could benefit from emulating?

You have a good point about emulating what is considered "divine" rather than choosing to use your free will to ignore the soul's messages to your consciousness about your chosen mission. But remember, achieving balance through karmic learning still is going on, and it's being accelerated beyond your understanding, so you would hardly consider all behavior as "divine" even if it is exactly in line with souls' needs, and you don't know what those needs are! As for the "divinity" of what you call "ascended masters," yes, they are higher in spiritual growth and knowledge because their souls never descended to the limitations of third density.

Matthew lived on Earth and it's in third density!

Suzy, Matthew's soul evolutionary status never descended to third density! He started out as a highly evolved soul and his personages in their various independent incarnate lifetimes haven't diminished that status of his cumulative soul. Well, in the truly "timeless" universe where All is Now, if one personage is dropping a bit, another is rising. [*The chapter "The Cumulative Soul" in* Revelations for a New Era *explains personage and cumulative soul.*]

I see. Are all the messages from the souls who are called ascended masters being received correctly?

Only in some cases, and understand this: I am *not* saying that the knowledge and wisdom in the *authentic* messages from them is not important! It IS! I'm saying that it's not necessary to go *through* them to reach God!

The well-intentioned channels who are not receiving the messages correctly are overlaying the transmissions with their *ideas* about separation, their own need to master esoteric knowledge as the means to reach their absolute conviction of connectedness with God. They are not deliberately misrepresenting the ascended masters. They simply don't know any better way, and they genuinely desire to help others find the same pathway they themselves are treading. It's not the best way, of course, because it's not the *direct* way.

Channels who have succumbed to ego aren't connecting with any source in the light and they're relaying the false information given by the lower sources they *are* reaching. In some cases, the messages are attributed to ascended masters, so you need to be discerning about which message falls into which category. Heaven knows how often we've instructed you all to be discerning about *everything* you hear and read! If you feel strong resistance to any information, that's a red flag from your soul—pay attention to it!

I do know that some messages attributed to the ascended masters actually are from dark sources, just like other disinformation is. Maybe it's how to influence "good people" to believe that if one hears "voices in the head," they aren't from God or any other "good" source.

This is not such a simple thing, the influence on "good people." It's as if there are two signposts that read "This way to hell" and "This way to heaven," but there's no signpost, "This way to real enlightenment and understanding and direct connection with your godself, which IS God." No, the only signposts are those heaven and hell directions within religious dogmas, and those were set up long ago by the little groups who wanted to control everyone else.

The lingering effects of those totally fabricated lies are fashioning the pathways of "good" souls who consciously feel they are following God's words, but actually they are being held mentally and emotionally within self-serving man-designed church rules. The mental is following the dictates of the various religions without questioning so they will "go to heaven." The emotional is feeling that if they deviate from what they've been taught, that is sinning and the price is, they'll "go to hell."

Remember the child who said love is with the heart, not the mind? The souls being born who are known as Indigo and Crystal children retain exceptional awareness of this simple truth. They know their God-Love connection, and to the great credit of the parents in most cases, these children are being respected for their innate wisdom. Eventually they will be heard by all who can shake loose from the dogmas, will understand why the dogmas were laid out for them, and will "see the light."

Are any souls here now really reincarnations of St. Germain or Archangel Michael or any of the other beings considered to be so high in the light?

The Christed light that is within every soul born into a physical lifetime is a new, inviolate, independent essence, Suzy—you've heard that often enough. The Christed light may be an *aspect* of one of those higher souls, to be sure, but to say that any person is the total incarnation of *any other soul* is totally incorrect.

What about the various soul growth stages? I've heard there are twelve—I think it's twelve—parts of the soul and each has to evolve in a set order.

Oh, *my!* A soul is a soul is a *soul!* It never is "in parts"— it is its complete own entity in fullness at *every* stage of growth. What is not understood is that the power of each soul enables it to be in all lighted space simultaneously, and the less a soul has evolved, the less of that ability it has.

Angels are different from the "ascended masters," aren't they?

Yes. Angels are collective beings of light, but they, too, are individual souls with names, missions and that same ultimate destination of reintegration with Creator.

The archangels and any other souls in the Christed realm are in a higher light status than God, aren't they? God Himself said so.

And He's right, of course.

So, is there a difference in the makeup of souls who are archangels and souls who incarnate?

The ingredients, you could say, are the same — the light that is the shining love of Creator and God. It is the amount of light within each that differs. It is not so that dark and light exist as two sides of a coin in all souls. In that highest realm next to Creator, ONLY light exists because those souls were created of light and never left it. When some willingly spiraled into depravity and deliberately made those pathetic monstrosities in your "myths," the darkness — as we'll call it for simplicity's sake — started, and those souls who did that no longer had angelic status. Darkness is no more than the absence of light, you know.

Yes, I do know that. Hatonn, how are you coming along with your multiple responsibilities as communications director and intergalactic fleet commander?

Communication is the more challenging by far because of all the wrong ideas folks have about telepathic communication, the DISinformation coming through, and that mountain of layers I was talking about. The commander function is *easy* by comparison! We're all in a holding pattern, performing our various technologies that are helping your planet recover from the eons of neglect and abuse and ignorance.

As far as settling in and identifying ourselves as your "space brothers"—including those of us who are living right there with you—your world is not ready for this yet. You're uncovering the darkness with each breath, and when all the uncovering is done that could pose a life threat to you and to us "aliens" popping in with our "space ships," we'll come. The same goes for those "aliens" who are walking your streets to properly introduce themselves. We're *all* eager for that day!

So are a lot of us!

We know this and rejoice in those souls! You will know ahead of time, you can be sure of that, and you'll be led to one of those landings. So will your son Eric, as "secretly" he is thinking that this would be for him the blasting away of his last little doubt that everything he has heard is fully the truth. Your other son and your daughter are not thinking about that at all—they're preoccupied with other mental meanderings and responsibilities.

Eric will be thrilled to know this. Hatonn, you have devoted a lot of time to me this morning and I thank you for this. Please just say "hello" as encouragement now and then.

Suzy, I *do* this! You *know* I do! I love you, my sister light being! Now I take my leave to tend to my other responsibilities. Know that while all are of extreme importance in this time of no turning back your clocks, none is more important than reaching Earth souls with the truth of their God-connection. The very essence of *life itself* is their connection!

A FARAWAY CIVILIZATION'S HISTORY

Janos

MATTHEW: Mother, I am happy to introduce to you Janos, who is from a constellation at the far side of the Milky Way as that galaxy's parameters are defined by your scientists. They see this area as a nebulous cluster, inseparable from many others at that distance. However, distance is not in your "light years," but rather in the universe's light *density*, and that would make Janos' homeland imperceptible to telescopes regardless of its location. This *is* a planet in the sense that it is a massive orb and rotates around a star, but it is not of the lower density of Earth in either physical mass or spiritual attainment.

The soul of their planet, like its population of souls — it could be no other way at that evolvement station — is at eighth density spiritual evolvement. The people are highly advanced in intelligence and also technology — some of the scientists are among those who have been sending their knowledge to Nirvana for filtering to Earth scientists. Janos' civilization has been formed by diverse populating origins, just as Earth has been. Now, Mother, please welcome Janos.

Suzy: Janos, hello! I am pleased to welcome you.

JANOS: My dearest greetings to you, mother of

Matthew. This is Janos now speaking. I have been told that you are a clear scribe and that I may speak to you about my civilization's history. Also that I may address you informally as Suzy. Please confirm if this is fine with you.

Absolutely, Janos.

Thank you. I believe that your homeland can benefit by knowing the history of my own. My people are named by our planet and it is one and the same name, Galatia. We have ascended from the lower fourth dimension and I know your world is currently ascending from third into fourth. That is why my information is intended to be valuable for your knowing and consideration as to how you can use my people's experience to benefit your own.

So many years ago in your counting that I cannot tell you exactly, my ancestors were a warrior people. They were not always of that nature, nor were they of lower fourth density spiritual and intellectual attainment. To start at the beginning, people of several civilizations who landed on our planet were attracted to its beauty and peacefulness and many settled there. At that stage of Galatia's evolution, it was similar to Earth, with large land-masses and many seas, and the planet herself was of fifth density. Harmony was the basis of life for a while, but eventually some members of one civilization wished to have power over all the others. The majority, who were being increasingly constrained, obviously did not want that arrangement to proceed. Discussions were not fruitful and thus the war scene came into being. As it continued, and *because* it continued, Galatia could not prevent her planetary descent in vibrations as it was in accordance with the energy being generated by her life forms.

At that time my people could live for many thousands of your years. Their bodies did not die because their DNA had no patterning for physical disintegration. Rather, they designed their bodies to best suit their selected missions, and when those were completed, they retired those bodies and manifested new ones in keeping with their new chosen missions. When they had accomplished all missions possible for their soul growth on the planet, they moved into lighter space for higher experiencing.

However, in the lower density to which they had fallen due to the tyranny, the development of lethal weaponry and then the onset of war, bodies were killed before the souls had completed their missions. This was such an abrupt departure from formerly that the population was severely traumatized. Billions of young bodies were being annihilated and the souls were in confusion, seeking other worlds suitable for continuance of their unfinished missions.

The pure in heart petitioned the intergalactic high court for relief, and this is the response:

As the free will of those who would plunder and destroy cannot be denied, those of you who oppose their rule must act upon your divine god-ness to generate enough light to dissuade them from continuing. Failing that measure, you may call upon God's higher beings to assist you with their light intensity and it will be given.

The pure in heart did not prefer to give higher beings the responsibility to assist and they declined to call upon God's stronger forces. Later they regretted that so greatly that as one voice, they cried out for assistance. It was given with that first request, but by that time the population was reduced by over one-half and the once-beautiful planet was in ruins. The abundance of light beamed to Galatia was more than the warring minds could bear. The battles stopped, but the warrior proclivity that remained in some souls caused their bodies to die, and the souls went to placements for remedial learning. The survivors were strengthened in spirit by the in-pouring of light that also was restoring health to their damaged planet.

With the horror of millennia of combat as a stark reminder of life on a planet starved for light, the people wanted Galatia to rise into dimensions where light was steady in its intensity. They learned that their desperate cry for help was answered because, by universal law, the power of their collective desire could not be denied. They actually had *created* the help they cried out for. They learned that each soul is responsible to chart its own way through self-discovery and self-determination, and the more souls who desired to live in the light, the more quickly that would be accomplished for the civilization. There were stragglers, to be sure, but the unison of thoughts in the majority slowly and surely lifted Galatia from lower fourth density to her station in eighth.

Your situation is much like that of the ancient civilization from which I descended, and like our planet, Earth as a planet is a living being composed of all souls who live upon her. Yet our planets are souls themselves as well, and if they wish to be free of their civilizations' free will destruction by exercising their own free will, they may choose to rise above it to the station where their souls came into being.

It is my knowledge that like Galatia eons ago, Earth has chosen to be free of the energetic baggage that would end her life if it continued. The laws of the universe permit planets to ascend out of their suffering that is caused by the life forms upon them, and those life forms must individually make their choices to ascend or descend. There is no middle ground. You have received messages that Earth is leaving that low density of spiritual awareness that permits warring and destruction to occur. It is now up to you individual souls there to act upon your own saving.

Suzy, may I request that you read this and if you wish, to ask questions?

Janos, I would love to read this. I have an understanding, but not the fullness of what you have said. .... Thank you. That certainly is an urgent warning to us! I thought that bodies weren't needed in eighth density. Or does the current population not have bodies?

They are not needed, but they may be manifested. It is the choice of each civilization, and in my own, it is the choice of each soul. Among my people are those who have chosen not to have bodies and they are in free spirit, yet they interact with those of us, like myself, who have chosen bodies.

Does each of you choose body shape, size and features or are all basically alike?

Suzy, I am amused and delighted that you think of this! Some conformity is observed, but yes, we each may choose within that so there is a grand range of appearances and all are beautiful to behold by our values of such. To a large extent, you inherit your appearance, and that is not so with us. Each soul chooses prior to birth.

All of that is so interesting! Janos, please describe the conformity you mentioned, and also is there any similarity at all to our forms or features? Are you a suprahuman civilization or something other than human?

By your measurement that souls of humans embodied beyond your evolutionary stage are suprahuman, yes, we are suprahuman and not of other genetic origin. Our conformity is in size and mass density. There is little similarity to your appearance except in height at maturity, which usually is like your tallest people, over seven feet, although less height may be chosen. Our girth at any age is very lean by your standards.

You would have difficulty seeing us in our homeland bodies if we appeared in front of you, but you surely would notice the bright shimmering light that would be evidence of our presence. It emanates from the soul in the same degree it exists in the soul. You call it an aura. It is in the colors of the aura that we have greatest flexibility, and that is determined by our choices of talents and missions and the extent to which we have accomplished them. My people appear in an array of magnificent colors, some unknown on Earth.

What you call features—coloring of skin, hair, shapes of noses, ears and such—are not evident in our people. The beginning civilizations had a large variety of features, we have been told, but we have none of those because we do not need them. Hair was designed as special protection for those body areas, and noses, eyes and such were designed to physically enable your five predominant senses. My people have continuous awareness of All That Is. We have no need for individual sensing mechanisms and enjoy far more sensing ability than exists at the density limitations of Earth.

We are androgynous in nature, which is the most developed balance of male and female energies. Both male and female members of my people have temperaments finely attuned to the universal order rather than the close identification with others of their gender, as you tend to do. There is little distinction between the forms of the genders at any age.

To give you a picture that would be representative of most of my people, I shall show you my image as I am in my homeland. I shall tell you that if we choose to travel to other civilizations, to thoroughly enjoy all the loveliness of those different surroundings, we manifest whatever body fits into that atmosphere most comfortably and is not startling to the native population.

Janos, I hope this doesn't sound unappealing to you, but what I see is a tall, slender icy blue luminous body shaped something like an ant standing on its hind legs, except that I don't see any legs. I do see long very slender arms and fingers. Am I receiving your image really badly?

On the contrary, Suzy, you are receiving it very clearly! The long slender arms with long slender fingers have functions well beyond yours. They are for accessing and putting into storage the universal knowledge that we have rediscovered up to this moment in our evolution. It is as if the entire body is a brain, to compare with your organ for storing memories of everything you have learned, and the arms are the conduits, or major entryways of additional learning that we retrieve from the universe. This would be like your most sophisticated computers that hold the many entries of information that you input. Some of our people, usually the elders, choose to have no arms. Their entire bodies can receive and simultaneously act upon information.

The stored knowledge is compacted within our bodies, like your knowledge is within your brains. The decisions about how to act upon our knowledge is inherent in our composition and could be compared to your minds—the thinking, reasoning part of you that works with the brain's stored information to decide the best course of action.

You saw correctly that we have no legs. They are not needed, as we move about only by the thought of where we would next like to be, and simply the image in the thought transports us to that destination. Still another way in which our civilization differs greatly from yours is in our creating of children, which is through the focused thought forms of the "baby" soul and the parents.

What you and we have in common completely is free will and conscience. Those are the birthright of every soul throughout the universe. Without use, the conscience loses its functioning ability and the consequence is demonstrated in the abusive use of free will.

Janos, you are the first civilization I've heard about who reproduce by thought forms! How is that done?

Only the parents and the soul to be "born" participate in the decisions about the new body. That is not to say that God is not involved, because each of them is a part of God. The decision-making is similar to the soul agreements made by families on Earth insofar as attitudes and aptitudes, but of course, not the automatic genetic inheritance. Also like your agreements, the soul first is made aware of growth stages yet to be accomplished to attain a balance in its experiencing, and based upon that, the soul chooses individuals who will provide the most optimal nurturing and environment.

When that soul finds two souls who agree to be the mother and father, all three focus intense energy upon a shared vision of the exact body the soul wants to inhabit. This is a co-creating process that starts with the "baby" soul's image that is projected to the parents. Although the image I sent of myself is a popular body form, any other style that equally serves the information gathering and storage purpose may be selected. The creational materials are universal elements that, by the power of the thought forms, are formed into the design and function of the image in them. Making a body actually is a simple and rapid process, Suzy—it requires only the clear image and the desire and intent of the three souls to manifest it.

That is mind-boggling, Janos! How does the "baby" soul find suitable parents?

At this level there are no secrets, yet there is privacy. Just as you have public records, you also have personal matters that are not known if you so choose. All souls who wish to have a "new" life in the family send out their desire, which is a distinctive addition to their auras, and all souls wishing to incarnate can see which embodied souls may have interest in welcoming them. So can everyone else notice this interest, but it is respected as these souls' private matters. Usually the "baby" soul has discussions with a number of potential parents before making a choice.

After the "baby" soul and parents make their agreement, does the "baby" inhabit the body while the three of them are manifesting it?

The baby's thought forms are inseparable from its soul,

so in that sense it could be said that it is "inhabiting" the body during the manifestation process, which itself is very rapid. What takes time is the collective concentration on the body design ideas so that all thought forms become exactly in attunement. A soul does not need a body for life itself, as that is inherent in the essence of every soul. It is only for experiencing physically what cannot be without some mass for functioning that souls choose to have a body of some sort.

Among your people, there is great misconception about "life" and the difference between a soul and a body. You have a process called "abortion" that some believe is the destruction of a new life, and there is argument about when a soul enters a body being formed in the womb. No *soul's* life ever is destroyed by ending the formation of a developing body. Bodies grow independently of souls through the natural laws of physical mechanisms reproducing in accordance with the cellular programming of each civilization.

Souls are not restricted to incarnating in a specific civilization. A soul's spiritual evolutionary status automatically puts it within a certain vibratory level, and it chooses a civilization within that sphere that can provide the experiencing needed for its advancement. The greater the spiritual evolvement, the higher the light station within which a soul may choose the civilization for embodying, or living as a free spirit member.

Souls whose spiritual growth needs are within the third density of Earth or other placements of similar vibratory status, have a number of choices regarding bodies. They may reside around the parents even before conception takes place, and after conception, they may enter the fetus to experience that growth sensation. If that kind of experience isn't needed, they may remain "outside" for other kinds of experiencing prior to the birth, but with a soul contract "claim" on the developing body that other souls respect. If a soul enters a developing body and then reverses that decision, the woman experiences a miscarriage. A soul may inhabit a developing body until imminent birth, then decide not to continue in that body and a stillbirth results. Also, a soul may make one of those decisions, experience what it requires emotionally, and in agreement with another soul, will exit and the second soul enters until miscarriage, stillbirth or live birth occurs. A soul with a "claim" on a developing body may permit another soul to reside in the body to experience the growth and birth sensation, then that soul leaves and the first one takes over the physical life.

These various situations *always* are by agreement with all souls involved, which of course includes the parents and any other family members, and the purpose is to permit chosen experiencing to several souls at the level they need. Abortion, like all the other stages from prior to conception through a viable birth, provides opportunities for the partic-ipating souls to experience the attendant emotions that fill voids in their experiences to that moment.

Bodies have a life force independent of a soul, and while it is an unusual situation that a body lives without a soul, this can happen. Souls have the choice to enter a cloned body or not, and if not, the clone still seems like anyone else because the brain and all senses and motor abilities are functioning. Another example is when injured or ill people are comatose. The soul may choose to remain with the body or not, and if not, as long as nourishment is given, that body continues to live in a vegetative state until it dies from deterioration of cells. [*"Human Cloning" in*

Revelations for a New Era *covers clones with and without souls, and the chapter "Soul Transference" explains souls' options regarding comatose people.*]

Suzy, I have seen and also felt your astonished reactions to all that I was telling you about my people, especially about our "birth" method. Yet at one time the bodies of my ancestors were much like your own and reproduction methods and souls' choices were much the same as you have today. To address your mind's question about the "time" for that evolution to happen, in your linear definitions, it could be considered billions of years. However, those definitions do not hold in the universe, where we actually are those ancient ancestors as well as being the souls we are in this moment. I cannot explain this in any way that you could comprehend that ALL *is* in this very moment.

You're right that I can't comprehend it, Janos, and I greatly appreciate your descriptions that we can relate to, to some extent. How many souls are in your civilization?

We are individual souls, not a collective soul civilization, so I can give you this with no difficulty for your under-standing—except for the number, perhaps, which is quite a bit to imagine. We are about five trillion in all, but that is counting those half or more of us who do not live on this planet Galatia but retain their presence among us who do. Although this is not an accurate comparison, please relate this to your family and friends who live a distance away or who are visiting elsewhere and this causes no changes in your feelings or images in memory. Of that half I mentioned, most are free spirits who may be anywhere in the lighted universe.

I can't imagine that number or a free spirit existence, but I can imagine that communication with them is telepathic. Is that so when you are with another individual or in a small group?

Yes, communication with our off-planet population is telepathic. We do have a language that is based on tones rather than a word vocabulary, but more often we "converse" on-planet by telepathy because it is the fool-proof means of communicating throughout the universe. The system of instantaneous translation of any language, including sounds other than word sounds, into the one universal language enables every soul to understand all others, so there can be no misunderstandings.

I have heard of that translation system, and certainly "no misunderstandings" is what is so greatly needed in our world. Janos, do you have a central government?

We do in the sense of orderly living and every soul participates in the process that achieves that. In no way could that be compared with your various forms of government, though, where people are elected or are self-appointed to function in certain positions and often make rules that do not necessarily provide the best for all the people. Our "government" exists because of our thought forms that create a harmonious essence throughout the planet and serves all of us equally. We have no written regulations or separate officers for some areas and different ones for others. It is an all-inclusive *sensation*, I believe may best describe it, that touches every soul here and every one flows within that. So you can see that we are free of the power struggles that once did prevail and led to near-planetary destruction those eons back.

I'd like to think that we will evolve to that point! Please tell me about family life.

Happily! We have very large families that you could call "extended" families. There may be hundreds of parents for each child insofar as loving attention and care. There is no quarreling about this whatsoever, as each adult offers but does not impose, personal knowledge gained from experience. This enables each young life the opportunity to choose from a selection of the many talents and accomplishments according to its own chosen experiencing and be free from indoctrinating influence.

Are there no small family units, only a mother and father and child living together in one home?

Yes, there are, but they are part of the extended family, like a community of souls with similar interests and affections.

Please tell me about your home and family.

Thank you for asking, Suzy! I do know all about yours and we will feel like friends if you know about mine. I would like that and I see and feel your pleasure in this. Here mates do not call each other an equivalent of husband and wife, which denotes a legal pairing, but rather a term that most closely translated into your language would be "dear chosen partner." This need not be a lifetime arrangement, and if not, it is agreeable to both. As I mentioned, there are no laws here that dictate any situations, and family unions are within the harmonious flow of our world.

Now, my chosen partner and I have been together for

nearly 1000 years. No, we do not "look our age," as aging in our civilization's DNA reaches a prime point of maturity in appearance and robustness of what you call "health," and beyond that point only learning takes place. We have two children, one of each gender. Our daughter Lila is over 250 years of "age" and our son Denos is 50 years "younger." Both have chosen partners and have very young children even by your age standards.

All of us are part of a community family that numbers over 1000 souls. Each set of dear chosen partners and their "young" children have homes of their own. These are not like your large buildings with separate units, but rather individual buildings designed for all to enjoy privacy. Although you could not see our bodies, you would see outlines of our buildings and I believe you would like the various styles, which are as numerous as the immediate family units because each family makes its home to suit its "nesting" ideas and interests.

You might think that this would make the community appear a "hodge-podge," but there is a unifying beauty in the diversity. There are no igloos or Taj Mahals among the styles as that would please neither any one family nor the community.

Suzy, I see you creating mental pictures of what my home might be, and you are not even close. You think of structures as solid walls with floors and ceilings. No buildings here fit into Earth architecture. "Walls" are translucent and move themselves when we wish to move beyond them without dematerializing either them or our-selves. "Ceilings" are iridescent skies or plants or flowers floating without roots or soil, whatever we delight in seeing. "Floors" shimmer as they ripple with our movements and issue forth magical music at our very thought of it. There are no windows yet sunlight is constant unless we choose a duskier atmosphere. If it is stillness and privacy we wish, the immediate area is a bubble of energy vibrations at a frequency that lets us disappear, like your fan blades. Yes, it is indeed as you are thinking — wondrous!

Janos, all of what you have told me is beyond my imagination — but then I don't read science fiction, so maybe a few of us wouldn't feel overwhelmed to know that their ideas actually exist in Galatia. You said that ancient civilizations had no death DNA programming, but does the part of your civilization that embodies eventually die and the souls go to your equivalent of our Nirvana?

No aspect of ourselves dies and so we have no need for a sanctuary realm like Nirvana. What we do when we have experienced the degree of balance required to move beyond this life is move to another world in the same or higher density that will offer additional learning opportunities. Our bodies served us well and we transmute their energy into whatever other form will serve the people.

How many levels of density are above you?

I don't know. I am aware that different schools of thought on Earth have decided how many levels there are and their numbers differ, but it is very unlikely that any could know something that even at this station we do not. We can tap into the universal mind and comprehend only in the measure that is to be our next level of self-discovery. To skip around would leave voids and create misunderstandings of All That Is.

I see. All right, a much simpler question: Are there animals in Galatia?

It is no surprise that you ask this! I have seen your dogs walking in and out of the room and taking turns lying at your feet. We have no animals in body, but we do have the energy of your animals that have taken the forms of whales and dolphins. This energy is the most spiritual of the over-all species on Earth. I believe Matthew has told you this.

Yes, he has. How do you know Matthew?

Ah! Suzy, you have little idea of how widely known and respected Matthew is! I'd say that few lighted souls do NOT know of him! I know some have told you this, but still you think of your "little boy" who couldn't possibly know as much as he tells you, yet you know that you couldn't be that creative in your thinking and writing. What you have done without realizing it is, you have achieved balance in this son-"professor" regard by suspending the need to understand, and that is letting you receive messages accurately because you just allow the transmissions to flow in.

As for how I know Matthew, just as you are thinking, our meeting was not for the reason that many others have met him, in his assignment as consultant and adviser for upgrading sanctuary realms. It was Ithaca who introduced Matthew and me. She, too, travels, although not nearly to the extent Matthew does. She was in Galatia to present a seminar, you could say, on the effects of music in healing. I've told you my people do not have DNA patterning for aging, and I meant to include not for injury or illness either, so it is not for us that several others and I wanted to learn from her. On occasion souls of other civilizations who have lost their way in astral travel are in great need of psychic healing, and it is these souls we are eager to help.

Matthew dropped in while Ithaca was here, and what a grand time we three had! One way that your son has not changed is in his quick wit and keen sense of humor that gave you such pleasure, which he mentioned to us. Both he and Ithaca are highly evolved souls, and while this was true of Matthew as your son, his service since departing his Earth lifetime has virtually zoomed him into higher soul station. You know that he has chosen to retain "residence" in Nirvana because of his love for Ithaca and Esmeralda. You don't know the vibratory level where his soul growth entitles him to reside for another incarnate or free spirit lifetime — it is high indeed!

Janos, I feel happy to hear that, but I am too 3D to know how to truly appreciate it. Sometimes all of this seems like a dream. Anyway, are any of your people living on Earth now?

Suzy, we *know* your feelings! No, none of my people are there at this time. Some have made journeys there in conjunction with other ET representatives on Earth — saving missions that were futile due to your nonresponsive governments — I could say, the belligerence and betrayals of your governments. None of my people were on the missions where some bodies were doomed in crashes caused by military interference and surviving crew members were killed or taken captive. It may seem that all "UFOs" are alien crafts, and that is not the actuality. Many crafts are manufactured on Earth using the advanced technology that was freely given to some of your governments, and those vehicles resemble elementary styles of *outer*-spacecraft.

Our crafts are impervious to any weaponry yet devised by Earth scientists. Laser, or scalar, weapons are catching up to the point where the smallest of our crafts at low altitudes could be hit, and this acceleration of development is being closely monitored. When Earth is within fourth density, that technology will be aimed at positive effects and no souls with malicious intent will be on the planet to subvert those applications. When the safety of that day comes, many ETs will arrive on your planet and those who have been living there all along will no longer have to hide their true identity. That will be a time of rejoicing!

A lot of us are eager for that day! Is your civilization giving us any assistance to bring it closer?

Our light intensity is forever available for sharing, Suzy. Not only is it not diminished by our sharing, it is intensified when it is received by any soul. It is not necessary to make this request to us by name. That is, your people do not need to know about Galatia or direct a request for help to us. All that is needed is for them to have in their hearts and minds the desire to live in love and harmony with others. That is the invitation to us and our light is instantly with those beings.

So a prayer to God or Allah or Creator or whatever name could reach you?

The desire in any prayer goes out to the universe. The energy of that desire attaches itself to matching energy and brings that back to the person who prayed, although it may not be in a recognizable form. What many of you consider prayer is not the full extent of the universal law. Every thought and feeling originating within each soul creates thought forms that operate according to this universal law. Although energy is completely neutral of itself, thought forms attach to its currents like tentacles and steer the currents toward like thought forms. The two matching types of thought forms unite and come back to the originator. When the thought forms are based in love, more love returns. Harsh, mean-spirited thoughts and feelings work the same way. This, too, you know about; however, perhaps this book's readers do not, and for those who do, it can be a reminder of their co-creating power in this respect.

But to answer your question more directly, it makes no difference which name is called upon to give aid or is given thanks. Light is without boundaries. All prayers reach the Source of this universe. The light within our people, like that of all others in lighted space, is instantaneously touched by all who have opened their hearts to receive it.

Light also is purposefully directed. Many, many civilizations, including ours, have the ability to direct light from any placement to those who are assisting Earth with their own technological developments. You know about some of these forms of help from the beings who told you themselves. [Revelations for a New Era *and* Illuminations for a New Era *contain messages from representatives of some of the other civilizations who are helping Earth.*]

Yes, I do. Janos, is there anything else you would like to tell me?

I can think of nothing, Suzy, and I see that you have no more questions. I will be with you as you prepare this transmission for the book, just as all others from whom you receive information are. If at that time you have more questions, I shall answer them.

I'm glad you came today, Janos. I am in such awe of your civilization that I think any questions I might have as I read all of this would be so trivial by comparison with what you have told me. But we'll see. Until then, my thanks for your message and goodbye for a little while.

Please do not feel that a questioning mind ever needs an apology. It is the minds shut in their certainty that have caused many of your civilizations to fall. I leave you now with great pleasure in our meeting and exchange of sensations and sentiments. Goodbye.

Many questions came to me as I was correcting my minor mistakes prior to printing, and, just as happens with all my other sources when I am reading their material, Janos came in. We had a much more relaxed visit the second time around, and as well as answering my questions, he expanded on parts of his original message. Most of our conversation is included here, inserted at the most logical place with a devised transition, and that accounts for any zigzagging of formality and ease in his expression that you may have noticed.

A REPTILIAN COMMANDER SPEAKS

Horiss

Suzy: Matthew, hello dear! Am I right or am I imagining that a reptilian commander will be giving a message for the book? That was my waking thought.

MATTHEW: You are right, Mother, and I am pleased to introduce Horiss, one of the commanders I met several years ago at a conference in Nirvana. He has been given permission by the Council to give a message for the book. That double "s" in his name indicates the best English sound, which does have a long soft "s" sound at the end, but please don't associate this with the hiss of a snake! In the language of his people, the various sounds of the names have a quality that is pleasing to hear. Now, please welcome Horiss.

Greetings, Horiss.

HORISS: My very warm greetings to you, Madam. I have been told that I may address you informally, but if you will, please grant me the favor to address you more formally as I will be more comfortable speaking that way.

I want you to be completely comfortable, and Madam is fine.

Thank you. It is known by some of your people that certain of my civilization are fearsome creatures that have been causing all manner of evil upon your world for endless time. We are not proud of that truth, and I have been requested to speak on behalf of our greater numbers who equally oppose the influence of those dark members. We, too, think of them as dark because of their actions, and we are in combat with them to rid their influence on your planet and all the rest of this part of the universe.

It is possible that of all who oppose their darkness, we are the most vehement because their actions reflect upon us as a total civilization. Those members are not in the majority and are not representative of the rest of us and it is not how we wish to be portrayed. Please let me advertise to your world the nature of the rest of us. Thank you.

Without intending to sound vain, I tell you that our intelligence level exceeds that of many other civilizations that also are advanced intellectually and technologically beyond you. We are less advanced spiritually than many civilizations that have not progressed to our stage of mental development. We are endeavoring to bring more enlightenment throughout our civilization and one pursuit of attainment in this respect is joining with others in light forces to subdue and then eliminate the dark reptilian influence.

All souls in this universe derive from the same One Source, Creator, which makes all of us inseparable aspects of Creator and each other. God has told you that He is the amalgamation of all souls in this universe and loves all in equal amount. I say God to you, Madam, because that is your name for the ruler of this universe. That equality of love is true from our experience, as we first petitioned to God to eliminate these most foul of our brothers from this universe. He has no authority to do this and likewise, no desire, because all subsequent soul aspects of those original ones are indeed elements of God.

The darkest souls of my civilization entered this universe from another in an energy blending of the two universes that was meant to be mutually advantageous by a sharing of light to advance spiritual clarity. Some souls resisted this opportunity and now in this universe, they have become God's responsibility to bring light into them. That makes it our responsibility to fight against their continuance in darkness.

Madam, am I going too quickly for you?

No, Horiss. All that red is typing mistakes and I'll correct them later. But I'd like to ask a question. Were the dark souls that entered this universe the original reptilians or did your civilization exist here and they chose to enter it?

I like your question, Madam! What entered was the soul energy with dark thought forms attached. It is not only the reptilian civilization in this universe that this kind of soul energy entered, but it is primarily this one. They were attracted to it through the universal law of like attracts like, and the attraction on this end was our civilization's inclination to see strength in maintaining powerful defense forces of great military might. The souls with darkness that are influencing Earth humans are the reptilians that have made clear to other belligerent souls that Earth is solely their territory in this conquest.

I see that your mind is satisfied and ready for me to continue.

The most effective way of eliminating the dark reptilians is by creating more light in this universe to the extent that their souls either will be infiltrated with it or they will leave here to flee from that possibility. No, I do not know where they would go as I do not know about conditions in other universes or if they can enter any without permission. That is why we are endeavoring to bring light to them here and now. Light is missing from those souls and they believe it will destroy them if they are in contact with it. It is their fear of that which motivates them to fight the light everywhere they see it. The light would fill them with the enlightenment they lack, not destroy them, but they do not believe this and so they continue their battle against it.

I would like to describe to you the light ones of the reptilians. Because you associate that name with your animal reptiles and have little affection for those, it is easy for you to picture us in those forms. We are not in those forms unless we desire to make them, which we don't, because those forms would be too confining for the movement and functioning we desire. We are at a level of intelligence where we can make any forms we design.

You have been told that the dark reptilians on your planet look just like any other human, so you know that all of us have that capability. It may be either pleasant or unpleasant for you to know that some of us with lighted souls also are there, and quite a number of you are genetically crossbred human and reptilian. This is neither to your advantage nor disadvantage, as this is DNA inheritance only and has no effects whatsoever upon your soul evolution.

Madam, your jolting energy leads me to ask if you would like to comment.

No, thank you, Horiss — maybe my energy is reacting to my seeing all those red lines on the monitor that indicate typing errors. But actually, I would like to ask a question —

are you here in spirit or maybe even etheric body?

Neither, Madam. I am able to see you distinctly from my homeland. At this moment I am in my "office," as a comparative term for your business management place. However, I do like your asking as it gives me this opportunity to mention that this ability to see at a vast distance is enabled by the likeness of energy bonding, which also facilitates your clearly hearing my words. I shall add that if I wished to be present in your office, I could be there in a twinkling either in spirit only or in a body that I would materialize. I would not choose to do this as I believe that a solid form abruptly appearing in any style configuration, even one familiar to you, would not be a comfortable experience for you.

I think you are right, Horiss, I wouldn't be prepared for that. Please continue.

Very well. Some years back in linear time, Matthew told you that we respect military power and do not hold much respect for a civilization that differs with that. In the universal "time," some of us are in higher stages of spiritual alignment and that higher evolved contingency of the "future" is helping us "in the present" to abandon that outlook. What our "present" members have believed is that the power of large forces is necessary to prevent invasions of dark-minded souls whose method of conquest is with military force. My people in majority are not invaders, but defenders. Now we are seeing that the greater light being generated throughout the universe is diminishing the areas under dark control, and this enables us to reduce our defense outlook accordingly.

You ask other civilizations' representatives about their people and I am eager to have you know more about my people. When I say "my people," I do not mean that we are representative of all reptilian populations any more than Earth humans are representative of all human populations in the universe. I am speaking now only of the people residing in my world.

We reside on a planet in this galaxy that is as near my solar system's sun as Earth is near Sol. We use the energy of our sun much more efficiently than you use the energy of Sol. Instead of your various forms of power generation, all of ours derive from our sun. Yours also can, and as you progress in awareness of this, that will come about. Also, there is no pollution from any source anywhere on the planet, not on the land masses nor in the seas, due to our technology that prevents such contamination rather than makes an effort to clean it up.

Our home planet is called Lacone [lah-conn—*with accent on the second syllable, which has an elongated soft "nnn" sound*]. It is as large as Uranus, to make a comparison that still is beyond your perception, but that tells you it is much larger than Earth, and it is about the same density of Earth in form and substance. We do not have the variety of natural beauty as does Earth, and which Earth itself no longer has in many areas due to environmental destruction. Our cities are larger than your largest. City living is the temperament and choice of most of us, and the union of ideas and desires focused upon the same goal manifested large, then larger population centers. Our cities are immaculate, as are all outlying inhabited areas throughout the planet. We can travel to any point on the planet almost instantaneously by thought or leisurely in vehicles.

The appearance my people has chosen when we are at

home or visiting other advanced civilizations is as I appeared in Nirvana, when I met Matthew. Male and female forms and features are much alike and with little variation in any. We do not have a mixture of races as you do and which creates the great variety in your appearances, but that is not the reason we are so similar in ours. Our collective choice is to look alike. Long ago we learned that differences in appearances can lead to prejudices and discriminations, and with our inclination to be a defensive people, we chose to eliminate elements over which we had control so that civil conflicts would not arise to weaken us.

To describe us, we are of a height not dissimilar to your average height, but we are uniformly slender except our females who are bearing children. The skin tone is pale blue-gray, which is pleasing to us although it is unlikely that you would find it so. Our most distinctive features are our eyes, which are large and dark. I know Matthew told you that they are so dark that you cannot see into our souls, but now he knows that is not so as he has evolved greatly since our first meeting several years back. To be more accurate, he is a highly evolved soul and through self-discovery has eliminated the layers of non-understanding that come with indoctrination of erroneous information and subsequent opinions or beliefs.

Our education is in line with our advanced intelligence and every soul is in the learning system from birth until the move onward to what you call death or transition. It is our intense desire for learning that has allowed us to give a back seat to spiritual development, and that is changing. Emphasis upon learning is as great, but now the mental is more balanced with the increased desire for spiritual, which is another kind of learning. It is the self-discovery I mentioned that removes layers of indoctrination and allows the opening of the truth of this universe and of Creator's laws that govern here along with God's laws about the order of celestial bodies and other such activity that is unique to this universe.

Our children are conceived and born in the same manner as yours, but their intelligence at birth permits speaking soon afterwards and fine motor skills start to develop immediately. So at a very young age, about five years in your time calculation but with maturity commensurate with your adults, they no longer are dependent upon parents for protective attention and guidance. It is the love of family that bonds us and results in our children staying close to home long after they are self-sufficient.

Madam, what else may I tell you?

Anything else that describes your life and your world!

My! I welcome this! Very well, to describe the planet further, there are many similarities to Earth, such as great differences in elevation, large seas, many forests and plants, barren areas of rocks and sand. Earth is more vibrant in its unspoiled places than our planet and has a greater variety of colors. Nevertheless, our environment is completely satisfying or we would make changes to more greatly please us.

You have in your mind structures, so I will tell you that our buildings could be considered sterile in comparison with the many styles and shapes you have built. Our preference is what you would call ultra-modern, I believe, with little variation in style overall but of course, consider-able variation in sizes in accordance with usage, such as residences, business centers and industrial facilities. Homes are decorated simply in keeping with the austerity of surroundings, and our choice of attire also is plain.

Perhaps from my skeletal outline, I am giving the impression that we are an austere, harsh people in feelings. This is the sensation I am picking up from you, Madam. While it is true that we are serious-minded and are not given to "frills," we are not without warm feelings. Our children are as precious to us as yours are to you, and our mates are the same. We are a monogamous people. Mates are judiciously selected and know each other very well before aligning as partners, thus separations rarely happen except by the death of one. We enjoy levity and many forms of entertainment in which a whole family is participating, so you know that the sources of amusement are suitable for even the youngest minds. Music is important to my people, and none of it is blaring and discordant noise.

We are well informed on events in many civilizations besides our own. Earth is of special interest to us, just as it is to many other civilizations of individuals and of collective souls, but it is by no means a self-serving interest. My people want the banishment of the dark influence on Earth to be replaced by peaceful means of living among all of Earth's inhabitants, and not to bring to you another source of troublemaking. Our military might in numbers and technology could subdue yours in a day, as a description of our capability. However, ours is solely a defense force, and its purpose to defend rather than invade is the vital element of difference between our two worlds. This is further proof of our warm feelings, which extend to civilizations beyond our own.

I see "government" in your thought. Our planetary form of government could be compared with Greek city states of your history. Not the warring with each other, but the equitable and benevolent rule that existed within each state is the basis of our planetary ruling body. We have the advantage of one language and telepathy, which provides clarity of expression and promotes honest communication among all the population. Smaller bodies govern large districts as this is more orderly and efficient in a world this size with a population of more than 20 billion.

Madam, do you have a question?

Would you like to mention the kinds of industries you have and other employment?

Yes, thank you. For our strong defense force, we need industries to provide weaponry and space vehicles and all supporting services, so we have what I will call factories even though you would not recognize them as such because of the technology of their production equipment. As my people ease from the stance of maintaining military might, there will be a transition from this type of production to others. This is in the planning stages.

Our emphasis upon education makes that one of the largest fields of employment. We have computerized education along with tutorial forms to present opportunities for our children to specialize in areas of their greatest interest and aptitude. This is equally available to our adults who wish to change from one specialty field to another. Studies are of our homeland history as well as the history of many other civilizations, and of course, all branches of science as it is in its authentic universal form. What you call "the arts" are of great importance to us, and I feel your surprise, Madam, although already I have mentioned fine music. Painting, sculpture, dance and poetry have significant meaning to us as an entire civilization. Parts of your world are threadbare in these necessities of soul expression.

Construction of buildings is by solid materials rather than manifestation by focusing on images. Although we could do that, and sometimes for expediency do so, my people find greater satisfaction in using their hands to form materials into desired structures and objects. This kind of productivity is a good balance to the concentration upon academic learning that everyone pursues. We respect the need for balance in our lives.

Many are employed in making and maintaining computer systems. I could boast of our advanced systems but boastfulness is not in our nature. It need not be as the condition of our world speaks for itself. However, I can tell you that our systems are at a development level that a word, even a thought, starts and stops operations and desired input or outflow are accurate and complete.

That is an advanced system! Horiss, you mentioned "death," so I would like to ask about the usual longevity of your people, and do you have a sanctuary realm that would be similar to Nirvana?

I did say "death" and only as a term of ease. The physical shell of us gets used up by deterioration of cells or by combat wounds, but we know there is no death—the soul has lived from the Beginning. But longevity in the physical shell when not cut short by combat is about 200 years. That is our current DNA programming, and it will change as we reach higher spirituality levels where physical shells can live much longer with full functioning abilities.

I do not intend debasement of our bodies by the reference to "physical shell." It is important that we have robust health to maintain combat fitness, and we do that, but I meant to make a clear delineation between the far lesser importance of our bodies as compared to our respect for our souls.

In keeping with that respect, we do have a sanctuary realm that is commensurate with our planetary population's advancement intellectually. That realm also is rising in emphasis upon spiritual understanding and attunement. I discussed this with Matthew at the time we met in Nirvana, and his sound suggestions for treating our most psychically damaged souls have been implemented with great success.

Madam, may I answer anything else?

Horiss, is there anything else you would like to say to the people of Earth?

Yes, thank you. As a summary of the intentions of my people, it is this: We do not often speak of our convictions and our nature, we live by them. At heart we are warm, peaceful, respectful and helpful, and that is what we look forward to showing you one of these days, when you are ready to welcome "strangers."

I think that is a perfect way to end your message. Thank you for coming today and giving such interesting information about your people. I look forward to welcoming you, Horiss!

And I you, Madam. I believe I will comfortably call you Suzy then. And for this time, I bid you good-day.

February 1, 2011

Horiss, warmest greetings to you! Thank you for working with me on those areas where a bit of clarification will be helpful to readers.

I am happy to be with you again, Suzy, if I may call you that. It has been more than seven years since we last spoke, and as we reviewed my message I picked up your question. Shall I answer now?

Horiss, I'm glad you're comfortable calling me Suzy. Since you know my question, please just go ahead and talk.

Very well! Yes, we have made satisfying headway in "lighting up" the reptilians in your solar system. Of course not us alone, but in concert with all the light coming from far distant sources and all the light beings surrounding you and those among you. It is to our great liking that some of the dark ones of our race have left your planet and by choice are being rehabilitated in spiritual sanctuaries, including Nirvana. We are diligently working to convince those remaining to give the light a chance and I cannot say that we are yet satisfied with the results of our efforts. Soon Earth will be in a vibratory plane where their bodies cannot survive, so you will be free of them by that means. We applaud that, of course, but our greater interest is in persuading them to accept light. Like other spiritually evolving peoples, we shall not rest easily until every member of all reptilian civilizations in this universe has abandoned dark proclivity. It is in the interests of all civilizations that we continue this quest.

I am pleased that my reply has warranted your smile, Suzy. If you have another question, I can't see it. Ah, now there is one: *Are any dark reptilians still on the planet leaning toward the light?* Not the most hardened ones, but those in lesser positions of power are wavering in that direction. No, I prefer not to identify any in either category, but you will see for yourselves as time passes.

And another question, so I shall continue. It is possible, but unlikely, that I shall visit Earth any time soon. My interest in the quest I mentioned along with assisting in programs to uplift my people spiritually are foremost. However, when I feel a sufficient measure of success, my family and I may vacation on Earth when she has been restored to her original beauty. And I thank you for inviting me, Suzy.

If we don't meet here, Horiss, I hope we shall somewhere, someday.

Suzy, maybe Galatia. I would be honored to introduce you to my homeland. And now, I bid you *hasta luego* rather than goodbye.

AN OLD FRIEND RETURNS

Lazarus

Suzy: Mash, dear, did I waken because I imagined you want to give me a message – or do you really want to?

MATTHEW: Mother, someone wants to give you a message. We didn't waken you, though, but since you are here and bright-eyed, would you like to take this now?

Sure. If not you, who?

An old friend! I'll let him introduce himself.

LAZARUS: My dear friend, Suzy, a very early good morning to you! Yes, as you are feeling, it is I, Lazarus. Isn't it wonderful to be talking again at your computer! I would like to give you an update of rather technological nature to let you know what my people and others as well have been doing for you.

As we last talked, many different civilizations have been at work to keep Earth stable during this upheaval. When you questioned Matthew recently about so many earthquakes around the globe – yes, of course we know that! – it occurred to me that you might like to hear from me on this. Not that my account differs from his, but we're all aware of the new book and I thought you might like to have my report to include in it.

Of course, I'd love that, Lazarus, and it's a wonderful surprise to have you back! Thank you for coming!

I'm delighted to be speaking with you again, Suzy! It's just as Matthew said—not in these words, though, because he speaks more delicately than I do—your bad egg scientists are at it again with "their" technology. I sent an image of "their" with quotation marks because it's not as if they developed this themselves. The Little Greys gave it to them in what was supposed to be a good exchange with benefits to them and to Earth, but as you know from Matthew, the Greys got a raw deal and so did you because the Illuminati has used that technology only to your detriment. We can't totally thwart their efforts insofar as manipulating your weather and making the earth quake and or volcanoes erupt—you know the deal with free will—but we certainly can reduce their expectations of widespread destruction and death toll. We lay down an electromagnetic grid that absorbs the kinetic energy and transmutes it into the ethers. The effect is somewhat like the ripples on a pond when you toss a little stone in the middle. Of course we don't get still waters to work with—what we do is diminish the effects of what the pond would do if a boulder had been dropped into it. And even with our softening act, Earth still releases the same amount of negativity that she needs to.

I have been counting on your help for many years, Lazarus, and it's good to know that you're still up there giving it. Is this a cooperative effort or are your troops acting alone in this?

It's a revolving door cooperative effort, with each of the

crews assigned to monitor Earth taking action in their particular sector at the moment energy leveling and dispersal is needed. When the force is more powerful than just volcanic rumbling or small underwater quakes, they don't need to get involved, but when something big is about to blow, the rest of the crews pitch in to whatever degree additional help is required. It's not just those geophysical events where we get involved, we also reduce the power of storms like your hurricanes and typhoons. We decrease the effects to the extent we can, but once those powerful forces above and beneath ground are set in motion, even our most advanced technology can't prevent all the disaster and deaths.

If Mother Nature were allowed to handle all of the negativity release herself, she would keep to areas where the least damaging effects would result and she wouldn't need our help. It's those maniac manmade efforts directed toward heavily populated areas where our help comes in handy. Let me give you an example, the hurricane that was named Earl. Mother Nature started that to release negativity out at sea where it wouldn't have done any damage, but the mad scientists got into the act—they intensified the winds into a major storm and directed it toward the mainland. That's when we all got into it—we decreased the wind force enough so we could turn the storm north and keep it from hitting the mainland. That was one of our more dramatic interferences and it buggered those folks who thought for sure they had conjured up a grand disaster.

Lazarus, I felt sure that we had a lot of ET help on that one and Matthew confirmed it. Thank you and all the others who did that—well, for ALL you've been doing for us! What else have you all been up to?

Well, we're keeping our eye on your rogues who try to send their nuclear warheads somewhere or other and we've vaporized a dozen or so of those—the warheads, not the rogues! Then there are the lesser aims in "black ops," as you call them, that we've stopped cold or seriously reduced the intended results. Some of us neutralized viruses in laboratory-made diseases so that the much-publicized pandemics never happened, and all along we've been reducing as much as possible the toxins in chemtrails, radioactivity in weaponry and other harmful pollutants. Oh yes, we also had a hand in saving the Gulf of Mexico from dying after the oil rig explosion.

And we're always on the lookout for meteors and other small celestial bodies and debris heading toward you—I think you'd be amazed at the number we've directed away from you. We aren't alone in this work. Almost all of us who are nearby have been in on this kind of protection that began eons ago, when Earth started descending into third density's vulnerable zone. I'll tell you about a relatively recent incident, a year or so before the turn of the century in your time. My troops weren't in on that particular save, but except for your civilization, it's known throughout the universe. An especially large speedy meteor was being directed at you by the peak of the dark forces—they had wearied of their slow-moving conquest of the planet and decided to just annihilate it. When your space brothers saw that this meteor had been pulled out of its normal orbit and redirected at Earth, they put out an immediate call to Menta's forces, who had the power to pulverize the meteor into tiny fragments that burned up before entering your atmosphere.

And we never suspected a thing—it's just as well! Well, maybe a few astronomers picked that up. If so, they must have been mystified when the meteor vanished.

If you could check with those who saw it, you'd find out that they discovered it just before it got nearly vaporized and concluded that it was an anomaly. You know that very few of your scientists give any credence at all to intelligent beings in space.

Isn't that changing?

Not significantly, but I can guarantee you that it's going to change in one wild moment when it's safe enough for some of our crews to land.

Isn't there a master plan for when this will happen?

Absolutely, as soon as it's safe for you and the landing crews. The Intergalactic Federation Council has coordinated this with all of us who have been roaming your skies for at least 60 years. Longer, some of them, and MUCH longer in some cases—for all its errors, your Bible does have some references to ET presence. You know Hatonn well—his Pleiadian-based fleet has been around a lot longer than most others, especially those in deep space who directed their powerful light in answer to Earth's cry for help several decades back and all of us who are nearby, relatively speaking, also got into the act and gave technological help. One of Hatonn's fleet's jobs for so many centuries I've lost count is maintaining the protective shield around Nirvana that extends to Earth during all visitations, residents there visiting you and vice versa—almost no one there is aware of these soul travels.

I know about that from Matthew. What ETs will be landing?

Along with representatives of the Pleiades, those from Lyra, Arcturus, Sirius and Vega probably will be the first because they are the ones in ships close by and also, they're your primary ancestors. I do know of Horiss' message, so you already know that some of you have reptilian ancestry, and some of their lighted souls will be coming too. I say "coming," but you know that many of us are there already. They will be ecstatic to reveal their true identities at long last, and some of them are going to truly shock you!

You mean because we know them so well by positions they hold?

That is exactly it.

I don't suppose you want to tell me who. Or do you?

No, because it's their prerogative to do this when it's time, not mine now. Actually, you might not be too shocked at some, Suzy, and we have to let it go at that!

OK, Lazarus. I'm so eager for all of this to happen! Is Earth in stable orbit or does she still need your assistance?

Our beloved Gaia…let me interject something here. Gaia is the name of your planet's soul, and ancient names of her planetary body are Terra and Shan, but we call her Earth just as you do even though it's simply putting a capital E on the earth that you walk on, which some unimaginative previous civilization did. It was the same thing with God, apparently because he is a god, not a goddess. Anyway, Suzy, yes, she has regained a great deal of her former strength with the incoming light, but we still are adding ours along with our technology to assure her stability. Not all the upheaval in ridding her of negativity is over, you know, and there's no point in diminishing our diligence in this respect until she is fully within fourth density vibrations. Then we'll all shout Hallelujah—our work there will be done! And at that point, you'll all know your universal brothers and sisters.

How is your family, Lazarus?

Suzy, you dear soul! My family is wonderful! Thank you for asking. I devoutly hope that when the first ETs make their presence known on Earth that people will be able to think of us like that—with families like yours, whom we love just as dearly as you love yours.

Many of us are so ready to greet you that way! Lazarus, it feels as if this is a wind-up statement from you.

Suzy, I'll bring my energy back just to tell you you're right and wish you a loving farewell for this moment at the computer. Let's "chat" more often, what do you say?

I'd love it! Thank you and your people for your steadfastness. Hey, have a great day!

———————————

Lazarus' name is pronounced with the accent on the first syllable. His previous messages as well as Menta's are in Revelations for a New Era.

PART VI

THE POWER OF LOVE

THE REBIRTH OF EDEN ON EARTH

Matthew

More and more, the peoples' voice is being heard in the universe as LOVE. Even when the word love is not being spoken, its countless expressions are permeating your world.

Our hearts are rejoicing because love is filling your hearts, and our beloved Earth—Gaia—is reflecting her joyousness in a magnificent light that is radiating throughout the universe.

Think of the ecstasy and wonderment of parents holding their first newborn child, a sensation that before experiencing it could not be imagined. Now see your-selves—collectively, you are bringing about the rebirth of Eden on Earth!

ALPHA AND OMEGA

God

To my children of Earth: You give me great joy! My final word to you in this book is that infinitely and eternally we are inseparable in abiding love. This is what I have been telling you all along—now you are listening and heeding.

The more love-light in each of you brings more to all of us. Each soul who finds this truth anew is another burst of love within me and thus within you all. We are not separate. We never have been.

While you may wish that I say something profound, I tell you that nothing is more profound than LOVE. It is the most simple, yet the most powerful of emotions. My Self lightens as each of you rediscovers our Beginning.

As it was then and ever shall be, WE ARE ONE.

Glossary

Angelic realms. Placements of love and light closest to Creator

Angels. Collective beings of light manifested by archangels in co-creation with Creator

Archangels. First beings created by Creator

Ascended masters. Very highly evolved souls

Aspect. A part of Creator, God or a soul that individuated for further experiencing

Balance. Goal and epitome of all experiencing

Christ. State of being one with God

Christed light. Manifestation of Creator's love, constantly available to all beings for soul evolvement and protection from dark forces

Co-creation. Process or product of souls manifesting in conjunction with Creator or God

Cosmos. The total of creation; sometimes used interchangeably with "universe" in reference to our universe

Creator. Supreme Being of the cosmos; also referred to as Totality, Oneness, All That Is, I AM, etc.; sometimes used interchangeably with God to denote Supreme Being of our universe

Cumulative soul. Ever-expanding composite of all experiencing in all lifetimes of its individual personages

Dark forces, darkness. Powers originating in deepest antiquity whose experiencing choices eliminated all light except a connective spark to Creator; foes of light beings and of the light itself; evil

Density. (1) In accordance with universal laws, dimensions of soul experiencing and spiritual evolvement descending from the pure light and love of Creator into total spiritual darkness; (2) degree of solidity in any form or substance

Energy. Basis of all life throughout the cosmos

Energy attachment. Positive or negative interpretation given the effects of any energy motion

Etheric body. Body used in spirit realms

Extraterrestrial. Anywhere beyond planet Earth; non-Earth civilizations

Free spirit. A soul that needs no body for experiencing a lifetime or one that knowledgeably accomplishes the soul's chosen missions, or both

Free will. Each soul's ability to choose and manifest lifetime experiencing

Godself. Each person's inseparable and eternal connection with God; also known as higher self, inner self, soul-self

Guardian angel. Primary celestial helper assigned to each person for spiritual guidance and physical protection

Karma. Cause and effect of a soul exercising free will; basis for selecting subsequent lifetime experiencing to balance previous experiencing

Light. Creator's wisdom, love and the power of love manifested in energy form; the most powerful force in the cosmos

Manifestation. Process or product of co-creating with Creator or God; the inherent ability and indivisible aspect of free will

Mission. Primary purpose of each Earth lifetime, selected for spiritual growth by the soul prior to birth of its personage; the selection by souls regardless of form throughout the universe

Negativity. In accordance with universal laws, the destructive forces initiated and expanded by negative thought forms

Personage. Independent and inviolate essence of a soul experiencing an incarnate lifetime; each contributes to spiritual evolution of its cumulative soul

Placement. Realm composed of various related areas for specific experiencing

Prayer. Direct communion with God through thoughts and feelings

Pre-birth agreement. Soul level agreement made prior to incarnation by all primary souls participating in a shared lifetime; agreements are designed for soul growth for all participants and are based in unconditional love

Reincarnation. Return to a physical life after a discarnate life

Soul. Spiritual life force; inviolate essence of each individual's inextricable connection with Creator, God and all other life forms throughout the universe

Soul contract. A soul's selection of experiencing in the pre-birth agreement

Spirit guides, guides. Discarnate beings other than angels who are our unseen helpers

Thought forms. Indelible and eternal substances produced by mental processes of all souls from the Beginning; the stuff of universal knowledge or universal "soup"

Universal laws. Parameters within which all souls experience and to which all are subject; also called laws of God, laws of nature

Universe. One of several such placements manifested by Creator and the angelic realms; a god or goddess is the Supreme Being who rules over each universe

OTHER MATTHEW BOOKS

Matthew, Tell Me about Heaven
A Firsthand Description of the Afterlife

Life in the world we call Heaven is active, vibrant and temporary. Matthew describes the reception of arriving souls, environment, relationships, communication, animals, reunions, nourishment, recreation, education, cultural resources, employment, pre-birth agreements, karma, post-life reviews, and preparation for our next physical lifetime.

Matthew Ward
1962-1980

Revelations for a New Era
Keys to Restoring Paradise on Earth

Through this book we can learn about our souls, the order of the universe and how thoughts create everything within it, the origin of human life on Earth and human cloning here, and who the reptilians are. Views from Nirvana of our controversial issues show the great difference in the two perspectives, and representatives of civilizations far advanced from ours tell about life in their homelands. September 2001 messages reveal what happened on "9/11" and in the aftermath.

Illuminations for a New Era
Understanding These Turbulent Times

God's descriptions of who He is give us more insight into who we are and the purpose of our multiple lifetimes. To help us understand what is happening in our world, topics of timely importance include Earth's ascension, why there will be no nuclear war, reasons for the invasion of Iraq, how we create our reality, media control, what love is and its power in our lives. More messages from other civilizations and more glimpses of life in Nirvana through Matthew's evolution provide further awareness about past, present and future in our linear time.

Amusing to Profound — MY CONVERSATIONS WITH ANIMALS
Suzanne Ward

What the animals in this book talk about shows that the range and depth of intelligence, emotions and comprehension in Earth's animal kingdom far exceeds what usually is attributed to any life except humans. These animals' comments — at times, with astounding knowledge, perception and sensitivity — will evoke smiles, amazement and maybe heartwarming memories or a tear or two.

The Matthew Books can be ordered through www.matthewbooks.com or your favorite local or on-line bookstore.

MESSAGES

Matthew's messages from December 2003 to date are posted on **www.matthewbooks.com**. Topics include current events in a universal context, the ongoing world transformation and spiritual renewal process, effects of planetary cleansing and Earth's ascension into higher vibrations, and what we can expect during the transitional period through 2012 and beyond, the era of Earth's Golden Age.